How I Live

Comfortably in Costa Rica

On a $ 1,000 U.S. Disability Check

How to escape poverty and live comfortably in Costa Rica

By Nathon Dees

This is a guide to getting the system to work for you.

While a diagnosis of mental illness or an injury can be a dream crushing death sentence for many, it can be a ticket to a more peaceful and productive life to those intelligent enough to listen to the valuable information that I am about to convey to you through my proven experience

Let's Begin.

Chapter One

Do you qualify and are you able?

There is no room for bullshitting yourself. If you don't qualify you don't qualify whether it is financially or realistically considering the depths of your disability.

If your SSI, SSDI, or Veterans Disability is over $1000 U.S. a month and you can function on your own with minimal assistance, but yet have trouble functioning within the Psychopathic Societal demands and physical difficulties of living in the U.S. there may be hope for you.

In 2003 when I was diagnosed with Schizoaffective Disorder 295.7 (Bi Polar Disorder on steroids) life as I had know it before had come to an end and I had some big decisions to make concerning my future.

Having no one to care for me or my children but understanding that I would be trapped into poverty in the United States with a very minimal future for myself or my children, I decided where my disability check would stretch the furthest and allow the greatest opportunity for my children to get an education and have a chance for success.

I Decided to Leave the United States where I was a mentally disabled second class citizen living below poverty level and existing on food stamps, and start living in a locked gated community on the beach in a tourist town and being able to buy real non GMO food and produce from a farmers market with the cash money left over after all of my bills and utilities are paid from my U.S. Disability check.

I am saving the U.S. government money, creating more openings in slum housing in the U.S., Using less food stamps and Medicare because I don't need them now, and most of all tens of thousands of tax dollars in VA Psychiatrist and Medications that I no longer need or use.

In the United States I was treated like white trash and forced to live in a slum and on food stamps. In Costa Rica I can take the same $1,000 a month disability check and have legal residency. I can afford to rent a place fully furnished with all bills paid and live like a real person with some dignity and honor in a more relaxed environment with less stress and less psychological demands.

It was the only logical conclusion for me.

Chapter Two

The Reversed Economics of it

Every time that I was successful in the U.S., I was penalized for it financially. The more I made the more I was taxed and the more debt that I created. It was a perpetual economic lie or shell game that could never be beat. After the unrealistic societal demands of living in the United State of Confusion caused me to have a nervous breakdown I seriously evaluated the realistic probabilities of ever having enough time and money to live on a beach or enjoy my life like the rich and famous.

Then I realized that the people that lived in those places were neither rich nor famous but they were happy and we paid big money to spend a week where they live and kill ourselves to wallow in the mire of American inner city filth.

I went to the Social security web site and used the Social security disability calculator to see how much money I would get if I just gave up on life and retired at 35 years old with the money that I had already paid in if I were to become disabled.

I had enough money for me and my two children to live comfortably in Jaco, Costa Rica at least until they reached adulthood and would be on their own.

At the time it only took $600 a month U.S. Pension t get a legal pensionado residency in Costa Rica, With my time in service in the Army and the Taxes that I had paid in as a contractor I qualified for $800 a month and I got $200 per child for my kinds giving me $ 1,200 a month to live on.

I moved to Jaco Costa Rica and rented my first place in Costa Bella for $300 a month fully furnished and all utilities with a swimming pool on the beach in a gated community with a guard and gardeners.

It was absolutely retarded financially to try and live in the United States and work for $20 an hour to pay $1,200 a month rent for an unfurnished apartment plus utilities and taxes and cars and insurance and Bills and fines and license and late fees and you get the picture.

I took the crazy check and I have been living on the beach in a tropical paradise for over a decade now.

Chapter Three

This is not a way out for Screw-up's

If you are too stupid to make it in North American society you will be just as stupid here too. Let's face it, if you are a fuck up changing places isn't going to help you and I personally don't want you down here and neither do the Tico's.

I've seen so many people that think they are going to come down here and make a new life but they never change the bad character that made them a loser where they were at, leaving them doomed to failure.

This book is for good people that got a bad break, not bad people trying to escape their wrong doings.

The drugs, prostitution and night life are too alluring for the weak minded and so many pathetic drug addict losers end up drifting through that it gets old fast. If you are a fuck up there, chances are you will end up arrested and deported here as so many of the dumb masses have.

You have to have a Police record report from the town that you lived in for the past six months as a part of your application process and if you are a loser and or have a questionable criminal background you will not be granted residency so don't even waste your time. This information is for decent people that have become disabled and not for idiots looking to escape the legal system.

Now if you are in control and you don't have an outstanding police record or tax evasion etc, there is a good chance that you could qualify for a life where you can afford a legal prostitute or enjoy some recreational illegal drug use in the privacy of your own home without having to worry about the Obama Marshall Law New World Order Police busting down your door and locking you up indefinitely with no questions asked.

It is all about balance. It is all about understanding and opportunities for those that qualify. You may be one.

Chapter Four

What does it really take?

Well we already covered the first two things, do you get a thousand dollars or more a month from the U.S. Government or can you get it?

Is the extent of your mental of physical disability at the point where that you can care for yourself such as day to day normal living?

If the answer to these two is yes then lets continue by all means.

Next you are not a sex offender, mass murderer, pedophile scumbag or so bi polar that you are a problem to your family and the people around you, and you can no longer work but given the proper constraints you can care for yourself. Then you might be able to pull this off.

I did, but I'm brilliant.

Being bi polar or mentally disabled doesn't mean that you are stupid it just means that you cannot function within the set standards of society as normality. Well just change societies. When given the opportunity to break free from the mind control programming in the United State of Confusion, it doesn't take one too long to realize that you were being forced to function in a dysfunctional society and that it is in fact that very society that caused the cognitive dissonance that created the structures for the mental illness that is dehabilitating you in the first place.

Now if you are physically disabled and you get enough social security and you qualify there should be no problem other than locating a small town that can meet your needs locally. Jaco is fully wheel chair accessible and most of the public transportation is also. There are also many people that offer simple services from Bank and ATM runs to doing your grocery shopping and cooking. You can almost roommate with a small family and have then care for you.

Are you a sissy and can you speak Spanish? If you are a lily livered French toast sissy in the first place stay home in the U.S.. The world does not need any more week frail materialistic Hipster individuals that have to have everything perfect. Normal Costa Rican living is not the same as modern convenience of the U.S. but that is what we are escaping in the first place. We are not coming here to change Costa Rica, we are coming here for Costa Rica to change us. It is third world living in many ways but there is no comparison between a third world paradise and a First World Slum! If you are on disability in the U.S. your standard of living is less than a middle class working Tico family. My twelve thousand dollar a year disability pension provides an income for two Costa Rican families and I have a better life than in the states.

If this New Life and hope for a future sounds like it is within your grasp I highly suggest that you learn to speak Spanish. Many of the people here are bilingual and my father still can't speak Spanish but if you are serious about this opportunity for a new life and future you should take the time to learn Spanish, at least common phrases and every day words.

Chapter Five

Do Some Research!

Hey folks I figured this stuff out while going through a divorce and experiencing a nervous breakdown. Hopefully you just have a disability and a life that sucks. All of the information that you need to pull this off is on the Internet and it is way easier to go through the process than it was a decade ago when I did it. Some of the fees and standards have changed of course but if the information is from anyone other than source its wrong any way.

I used an association of residents to help me with the process. The A.R.C.R... They had their own attorneys and all they did was take care of the needs of their members who were all foreign residents living legally in Costar Rica. I joined their organization and paid their annual fee of $100 at the time and they provided me with everything that I needed to do step by step. I followed their instructions and saved my money and after no time at all I was a legal pensionado residente with a cedula in my hand.

The rest was up to me. All I had to do was follow the banking instructions that they gave me and exchange so many U.S. dollars per month into C.R. Colones and keep record of it, Join the social security program and pay the monthly fee of about $14 (the Caja) for medical coverage, and stay out of trouble.

I found all of this out over the internet just by doing research, then I started focusing on studying about Costa Rica and determining what area would best suit my own personal needs.

Chapter Six

Arrange a scouting trip.

By the time that the ink was dry on my divorce papers I had a ticket to Costa Rica.

I had mapped out every area that I had studied and I was personally walking the streets of the towns to see where I felt comfortable. My Friend Art and I walked all over San Jose and Escazu, Heredia and Santa Anna. We had toured the central valley and saw many really cool places to live for way cheap. You could easily live around San Jose and have everything that you needed and a nice place to live but that's not what I was looking for.

The first stop on the Pacific coast from the Coca Cola bus terminal in San Jose is Jaco, Costa Rica. The jewel of the Pacific Coast and the Las Vegas of Central America, I had found my new home!

Jaco had every convenience of a ritzy tourist town on the beach but yet was still a stone's throw away from the real Costa Rica. Five miles North you could go World Class Sports fishing at the Los Suenos Marina and Resort Hotel and five miles south you could ride overhead barrels at the world Famous Hermosa Beach and party at the backyard.

Jaco offered everything from sky scraper condos on the beach to quaint little Tico houses and apartments as well as Hostel, Hotels and apartments of all price ranges.

With very little effort I made contact with the land lord of one of the properties that I had viewed and made all the rental arrangements for the first six months as soon as I returned to the states to make preparations for my new life.

Chapter 7

Making the big Move

Once I had made the mental commitment and covered all of my bases there was really nothing to it but to do it. It was much simpler than you may think.

The hardest things were dealing with my own issues. I had to get a clear title to my kids and get permission to leave the country with them. I also had to have every kind of school and medical record known to mankind for my kids. If you don't have kids or pets you are home free.

I had to have good legal documents and everything stamped properly and notarized but other than that I just needed to liquidate all of my crap, get on a plane, and start my new life.

One of my friends was arguing with my dad about what we should sell, give away or take. I took a $700 Fender Acoustic 12 string guitar and smashed it up against a stone wall and said "That's how I'm packing! I don't need any of this junk!" of course the guitar could have been sold but I was making a point. I have moved to Costa Rica three times and all that I brought with me each time was a Marshall 50 watt combo and my 1974 Fender Stratocaster and one backpack of shorts and T shirts.

You Don't need anything!!! I cannot stress this enough!

You are not a millionaire taking your prized collection with you, you are a disabled person trying to escape poverty and mass extermination once the Marshal Law takes effect in the United States. Once they start implementing Agenda 21 and exterminating the homeless and mentally ill in FEMA camps, you will be glad to have escaped with a suitcase and backpack of personal items.

This really is about creating a functional reality for yourself and not about materialism, greed or attachment to the North American way of life. This is about an opportunity to leave behind the plastic molded fake reality that you never fit into in the first place and becoming the real person that you were created to be.

If you are not willing to walk away from the lie and live life as a real human than you can just stay a member of a dying cancerous empire while I use the last remaining funds left that I paid into the system to enjoy a simple life of peace and luxury away from the toxic society that affords me this paradise. Many are called but few will answer and great is the path of the Dumb Masses and many are they, but narrow is the path of those with their heads out of their ass and they deserve a free ride just because everyone else is so fucking stupid and all of the money is going to be gone anyway sooner or later.

Chapter Eight

Settling in, in Jaco

We arrived at night to a home that we had only seen one time and had left everything that we knew behind.

 Just me and my two children and our friend that had moved with us that had lived in Costa Rica previously. By networking I had found another person that had not only lived in Costa Rica before and new the ropes a little, but could also speak Spanish and was returning to live in Costa Rica.

I offered him a room in my house until I could get on my feet and he could do the same. His name is Chuck and he is a complete bum that just mooches off people and lives here illegally but yet with a guitar, a song, and a smile he schmoozed his way into a comfy gig in Manuel Antonio and never returned to the United States accept to bum money off of his family members.

I was more worried about the kids fitting in and getting along. By the first morning they had met all of the local kids and Aaron was out surfing with our new neighbors Axel and Sean. All of the other Neighbors started bringing us gifts and weed and we had a party on the front porch the very first night after we had arrived to our new home in Jaco Costa Rica. After over ten years I still see my very first neighbors from Costa Bella on regular bases in Jaco. They always ask about my children and we reminisce about my early days in Jaco.

It took very little time to shake off the funk left on us from the New world Order Mind Control Programming and start living a life as normal human beings again, but not long at all after we arrived we soon forgot everything about the non sustainable commercial reality that we had been living in.

We had made it, and I had not only rescued my children and protected myself from being institutionalized, I paid for it with the very money that was funding the destruction of the American way. I used what they had created for my demise to save myself and afford a future for my kids.

Chapter Nine

So what are you waiting for?

In the years that are ahead of us in the U.S. things are going to get much worse before they get better.

 Once the economic collapse takes place no will be getting out.

If you are a mentally disabled veteran or a poverty stricken disabled person you are already on a list of people to be taken out once the Marshall Law commences in the States. If you have your money going to direct deposit you can go to the U.S. Embassy and inform the IRS that you are here once you are settled in and you will be off the radar for good. You can even have your U.S. Treasury check directly deposited into your Costa Rican bank account and automatically transferred into colons (the national currency).

I was afraid about having to go back in for reevaluations and test every so many years. It never happened. I went back to the states and tried again to fit in and ended up getting thrown in a maximum security U.S. Government military psycho ward for six days for no apparent reason.

I went in to tell them that I was doing better and they said that I was narcissistic and delusional for thinking that I was better, so I left and came back to paradise never to return to the United State of Confusion again.

Leaving the United States was the best thing that ever happened to me and the same money would not have done squat for me back home in the States. I used this time of healing and reflection to write a book series and help other people that suffer from the same affliction as I do. I have taken what was given me and done the absolute most that I could with it and I can only hope that it inspires you to see the possibilities that lay ahead for you too if and when you apply your selves.

Now the Complete Story

What I did and How I did it

From the Beginning

SATAN

GOD

OR

SCHIZOAFFECTIVE

DISORDER 295.7

The life and times of
TEXAS GUITAR LEGEND NATHON DEES

SATAN

GOD

OR

SCHIZOAFFECTIVE

DISORDER 295.7

The life and times of
TEXAS GUITAR LEGEND NATHON DEES

This is the true story of one man's amazing struggle with reality, religion and mental illness. As you read you will join in with Texas Guitar Legend Nathon Dees as he takes you on an adventure of his life and how he finally broke free from a Christian society and learned to cope with de habilitating mental illness in a unique and interesting way.

SATAN, GOD OR SCHIZOAFFECTIVE DISORDER 295.7

THE LIFE AND TIMES OF TEXAS GUITAR LEGEND NATHON DEES

INTRODUCTION

My name was once the Rev. Nathon Q. Dees, former Associate Pastor of the First Baptist Church of Sheldon, in my home town of Sheldon, Texas, an alumni of The Abundant Life School of Ministry, a prospective member of the Alliance Christian motorcycle ministry and a Free Mason. I was a self employed veteran and held a license for home building, construction, remodeling, renovations, waste water systems and owned a custom motorcycle shop.

Now my I'm just plain old Nathon living from day to day on a beach in Jaco, Costa Rica on a US government pension check for being mentally disabled as the result of Schizoaffective Disorder 295.7 as defined by the DSM IV.

I delivered myself from Satanic possession, Demonic oppression, angels, devils, heaven, hell and the church but it cost me everything including my wife, friends and even my country to know and accept the fact that I was mentally ill and that everything that I believed was a delusion caused by my illness and perpetuated by the lies of Christianity and society in the U.S..

Now that I've traded theology books and bibles for psychology and philosophy books it is very clear to me that I was mentally ill even as a small child and the events of my youth that led to my salvation were textbook undiagnosed mental illness. I spent fifteen years of my life institutionalized in the church before I realized that I was sick and needed help, not ancient fairy tells that allowed me to live within a completely delusional world created by the myths of Christian doctrine and folklore.

Schizoaffective disorder 295.7
Definition
Schizoaffective Disorder is basically a cross between a disturbance in thought and a disturbance in mood. Both symptom clusters (depressive/manic and schizophrenic) must exist at the same time (co morbid) to justify a diagnosis of this disorder.
Diagnostic criteria
A. An uninterrupted period of illness during which, at some time, there is either:
☐ (1) a Major Depressive Episode,
☐ (2) a Manic Episode, or
☐ (3) a Mixed Episode

Concurrent with symptoms that meet (4) Criterion A for Schizophrenia.
Note: The Major Depressive Episode must include depressed mood.
(1) Criteria for Major Depressive Episode Five (or more) of the following symptoms have been present during the same 2-week period and represent a change from previous functioning; at least one of the symptoms is either (1) depressed mood or (2) loss of interest or pleasure. **Note:** Do not include symptoms that are clearly due to a general medical condition, or mood-incongruent delusions or hallucinations.
☐ depressed mood most of the day, nearly every day, as indicated by either subjective report (e.g., feels sad or empty) or observation made by others (e.g., appears tearful). Note: In children and adolescents, can be irritable mood.
☐ markedly diminished interest or pleasure in all, or almost all, activities most of the day, nearly every day (as indicated by either subjective account or observation made by others)
☐ Significant weight loss when not dieting or weight gain (e.g., a change of more than 5% of body weight in a month), or decrease or increase in appetite nearly every day. Note: In children, consider failure to make expected weight gains.
☐ Insomnia or hypersomnia nearly every day
☐ Psychomotor agitation or retardation nearly every day (observable by others, not merely subjective feelings of restlessness or being slowed down)
☐ Fatigue or loss of energy nearly every day
☐ Feelings of worthlessness or excessive or inappropriate guilt (which may be delusional) nearly every day (not merely self-reproach or guilt about being sick)
☐ diminished ability to think or concentrate, or indecisiveness, nearly every day (either by subjective account or as observed by others)
☐ Recurrent thoughts of death (not just fear of dying), recurrent suicidal ideation without a specific plan, or a suicide attempt or a specific plan for committing suicide

The symptoms do not meet criteria for a Mixed Episode
The symptoms cause clinically significant distress or impairment in social, occupational, or other important areas of functioning.
The symptoms are not due to the direct physiological effects of a substance (e.g., a drug of abuse, a medication) or a general medical condition (e.g., hypothyroidism).
The symptoms are not better accounted for by Bereavement, i.e., after the loss of a loved one, the symptoms persist for longer than 2 months or are characterized by marked functional impairment, morbid preoccupation with worthlessness, suicidal ideation, psychotic symptoms, or psychomotor retardation.
(2) Criteria for Manic Episode A distinct period of abnormally and persistently elevated, expansive, or irritable mood, lasting at least 1 week (or any duration if hospitalization is necessary).

During the period of mood disturbance, three (or more) of the following symptoms have persisted (four if the mood is only irritable) and have been present to a significant degree:

☐ inflated self esteem or grandiosity

☐ decreased need for sleep (e.g., feels rested after only 3 hours of sleep)
☐ More talkative than usual or pressure to keep talking
☐ Insomnia or hypersomnia nearly every day
☐ Psychomotor agitation or retardation nearly every day (observable by others, not merely subjective feelings of restlessness or being slowed down)
☐ Flight of ideas or subjective experience that thoughts are racing
☐ Distractibility (i.e., attention too easily drawn to unimportant or irrelevant external stimuli)
☐ Increase in goal-directed activity (either socially, at work or school, or sexually) or psychomotor agitation
☐ Excessive involvement in pleasurable activities that have a high potential for painful consequences (e.g., engaging in unrestrained buying sprees, sexual indiscretions, or foolish business investments)

The symptoms do not meet criteria for a Mixed Episode
The mood disturbance is sufficiently severe to cause marked impairment in occupational functioning or in usual social activities or relationships with others, or to necessitate hospitalization to prevent harm to self or others, or there are psychotic features.
The symptoms are not due to the direct physiological effects of a substance (e.g., a drug of abuse, a medication, or other treatment) or a general medical condition (e.g., hyperthyroidism).
(3) Criteria for Mixed Episode The criteria are met both for a Manic Episode and for a Major Depressive Episode (except for duration) nearly every day during at least a 1-week period.
The mood disturbance is sufficiently severe to cause marked impairment in occupational functioning or in usual social activities or relationships with others, or to necessitate hospitalization to prevent harm to self or others, or there are psychotic features.
The symptoms are not due to the direct physiological effects of a substance (e.g., a drug of abuse, a medication, or other treatment) or a general medical condition (e.g., hyperthyroidism).
(4) Criterion A for Schizophrenia Two (or more) of the following, each present for a significant portion of time during a 1-month period (or less if successfully treated):
☐ Delusions
☐ Hallucinations
☐ disorganized speech (e.g., frequent derailment or incoherence)
☐ Grossly disorganized or catatonic behavior
☐ Negative symptoms, i.e., affective flattening, alogia, or avolition

Only one symptom is required if delusions are bizarre or hallucinations consist of a voice keeping up a running commentary on the person's behavior or thoughts, or two or more voices conversing with each other.
B. During the same period of illness, there have been delusions or hallucinations for at least 2 weeks in the absence of prominent mood symptoms.

C. Symptoms that meet criteria for a mood episode are present for a substantial portion of the total duration of the active and residual periods of the illness.

D. The disturbance is not due to the direct physiological effects of a substance (e.g., a drug of abuse, a medication) or a general medical condition.

Specify if:

☐**Bipolar Type:** if the disturbance includes a Manic or a Mixed Episode (or a Manic or a Mixed Episode and Major Depressive Episodes)

☐**Depressive Type:** if the disturbance only includes Major Depressive Episode

Associated features

☐ Learning Problem
☐ Hypoactivity
☐ Psychotic
☐ Euphoric Mood
☐ Depressed Mood
☐ Somatic/Sexual Dysfunction
☐ Hyperactivity
☐ Guilt/Obsession
☐ Odd/Eccentric/Suspicious Personality
☐ Anxious/Fearful/Dependent Personality
☐ Dramatic/Erratic/Antisocial Personality

CHAPTER ONE
IN THE BEGINNING THERE WAS SCHIZOPHRENIA

I was born on June the second 1967 the fifth pregnancy of an RH incompatible couple.

RH incompatibility has links to Schizophrenia. This is a condition where the mother's blood attacks the father's blood within the fetus, it doesn't affect the first child but it gets progressively worse each additional birth. Medicine had overcome this condition completely by the early seventies in the US.

My mom Jody who suffered from severe depression her whole life and my dad Byron who had young adult schizophrenia with hallucinations by his early twenties. I gathered this by the stories he would tell me of seeing and talking to his spirit self when he worked on the dredge boat at night. I attributed the story to the fact that he was a messenger that turned away from God.

He was no less than a genius but had a really twisted perspective of life and the most grandiose self image of anyone you'd ever meet, not just self confident but more God like passing judgment on the world for being less than he was. My father was a very successful self employed business owner with one of the largest electric motor repair and machine shops in Texas, as well as motels, apartments, A/C and electrical companies, rental properties, ice cream parlors, home building and construction companies you name he did it at least once. He was a veteran, a former sheriff's deputy, a Free Mason and a Rotarian.

His mental illness gave him incredible abilities and vision but also added an equal amount of problems but like many who never see a doctor or have a breakdown he used denial therapy. His power of persuasion is so strong that you could be standing there with him and see something happen and he'd ask you if you were sure it really happened in a way that would make you doubt yourself.

My mom Jody had been abused psychologically as a child by her father who was a Christian, which gave her a disliking of religion and hatred towards most men especially my father. She was a good and faithful wife and mother who longed for the day when she could be left alone by everybody and finally just sit and read books which she loved to do. Mom hated Christmas which I agree with. She was and still is the most non bullshit person that I have ever met.

Mom understood that we all had problems and told us to deal with it. I'll never forget the day she told me that she always believed that I would be the child that killed myself. My mom warned me to keep my guard up against suicidal thoughts.

My mom had five pregnancies, first my brother Robert who was a little wild as a teen but after that got married and led a productive and normal life. Robert was a Free Mason and a self taught engineer. My brother Robert was a brilliant and honorable man, He died of cancer at the age of forty nine. He is survived by his wife Patty and his two children Carrie and Chase.

Next, my sister Sherrill who was kind, beautiful and smart, she excelled in school and has made a lifelong career out of learning and going to college. Sherrill was born RH incompatible and had three blood transfusions at birth to stabilize the condition.

Sherrill has Bi Polar 1 disorder and has spent thousands of dollars on doctors and psychiatrist that did more harm than good. She rebounds back and forth from religion to holistic medicine, she is brilliant and a visionary but her life is an emotional roller coaster. One of the reasons that Sherrill was never hospitalized is because her husband Danny is a good man that has always supported her and put up with the illness. They have three children, Twins Lauren and Danny Jr. and a younger daughter named Madison. Byron and Jodie's third child was Damon, who was very special, He had problems like, lazy eye, dyslexia and ADD he was off the scale from the start. He was a hyper active Tasmanian Devil who had been kicked out of school for good by fourteen years old and asked never to come back after bringing a fire arm to school. Damon has been a complete drug addict and alcoholic since thirteen and has been through the best rehabilitation programs in the US. Damon was a thief and a compulsive liar, he has been in prison fifteen of the last twenty years and is currently living in a hospital for drug treatment.

The last we heard he was in a rehab center in Florida and back on his meds. Having Damon as a part of my life has been an absolute and complete terror every since I can remember. For instance; how many times have you had to hold your own drug crazed brother off at gun point or turn him into the police to protect your family? The next pregnancy, the fourth was a late term miss carriage resulting from the increasing RH incompatibility factor in my mom's blood.

Next was me, Nathon the fifth and final child, in fact my mom not only got her tubes tied but she basically stopped having sex. By this time the doctors knew a lot more about RH incompatibility and with my mother's medical history they where prepared for the worst. I was born three weeks pre mature and dying from my own blood. My father took me from the hospital and drove me to The Texas Children's Hospital's special care unit himself with my aunt Mary holding my blue dying body in her arms. At Texas Children's I received thirteen complete blood transfusions before my condition stabilized, every time the RH factor would reach eighteen they would start the process over. On the final attempt my RH level reached twenty one and subsided. My father was told by the doctors that there was a great possibility that I would be mentally ill, either mentally retarded or brilliant but with some problems, I guess I've been both.

"Hemolytic disease of the newborn, also known as **hemolytic disease of the fetus and newborn, HDN, HDFN,** or **erythroblastosis fetalis**,[1] is an alloimmune condition that develops in a fetus, when the IgG molecules (one of the five main types of antibodies) produced by the mother pass through the placenta. Among these antibodies are some which attack the red blood cells in the fetal circulation; the red cells are broken down and the fetus can develop reticulocytosis and anemia. This fetal disease ranges from mild to very severe, and fetal death from heart failure (hydrops fetalis) can occur. When the disease is moderate or severe, many erythroblasts are present in the fetal blood and so these forms of the disease can be called *erythroblastosis fetalis* (or *erythroblastosis foetalis*).

Hemolysis leads to elevated bilirubin levels. After delivery bilirubin is no longer cleared (via the placenta) from the neonate's blood and the symptoms of jaundice (yellowish skin and yellow discoloration of the whites of the eyes) increase within 24 hours after birth. Like any other severe neonatal jaundice, there is the possibility of acute or chronic kernicterus. Profound anemia can cause high-output heart failure, with pallor, enlarged liver and/or spleen, generalized swelling, and respiratory distress. The prenatal manifestations are known as hydrops fetalis; in severe forms this can include petechiae and purpura. The infant may be stillborn or die shortly after birth.

CHAPTER TWO
WHAT DID YOU REALLY EXPECT?

Nathon Dees and Mother Joan Dees

Bad blood and poor genetics. It's a good thing we marry for love and looks.

I was already a candidate from genetic inheritance to receive Depressive Bi Polar 2 Disorder from my mom and Young Adult Schizophrenia from my dad.

Not to mention a long history of doctors, priest, pedophiles, murderers and womanizers on both sides of the family. Thanks mom and dad! Now that they had children together I also had a blood disorder that causes retard fetal brain development forming an enlarged neuro vascular system.

I was messed up from the beginning but I guess things could have been much worse.

You know that's the thing with Schizophrenia, ten fingers, ten toes, perfectly normal on the outside and usually extremely intelligent. Who is trying to diagnose a problem with a perfectly healthy child that's bright and happy and has a great imagination?

Even now as an adult I find that since I'm articulate and can communicate with some degree of intelligence people find it hard to believe that I am mentally ill. I have Schizoaffective Disorder 295.7 tattooed on my fore arm and people still don't believe me. I guess mentally ill people are supposed to be stupid, retarded or John Nash before people can accept or understand it. Furthermore it is impossible for a charismatic Christian to accept my illness because it challenges their faith. In retrospect, I feel that I could have been committed to an institution on believing in Christian doctrine alone. The DSM-IV has a section on religious related mental illness that address these issues and rename schizo related symptoms that occur in religion so as not to condemn the religious community to mental illness. I call a duck a duck and schizophrenia is schizophrenia whether in a cultural religious context or not.

I am thankful that there are dedicated healthcare professionals that know and understand what true mental illness is.

CHAPTER THREE
EARLY CHILD HOOD SURVIVAL GUIDE

I had a good family and a happy childhood, my parents didn't even smoke or drink. We had the makings of a normal family but we were a really strange. We just never really did things like the other kid's families did and everyone seemed to talk bad about each other when the other folks weren't around. My parents weren't abusive or anything and the only real terror in our life was Damon whom I'm still convinced was spawned by Satan.

I remember watching children's programming on PBS and thinking that I was supposed to be on those TV shows, I knew someone was searching for me at that very moment, that I was somehow special. I had talent, I could sing and dance and I was smart. in fact; " too smart for my own good" is what I remember them saying about me. When Mr. Rogers would come on TV and encourage us to go to the world of make believe I was already there. I took many trips on Charley the trolley. My imagination was so powerful that everything was real to me. I was afraid of Spider man and Oscar the grouch, and I taught myself to spell watching children's programming on PBS. I would spend hours laying in my front yard looking for four leaf clovers knowing that if anyone could find the way to Brigadoon it was me or laying in the yard with mirrors and my dad's Chariots of the God's book trying to contact aliens so they could find me.

I also remember clearly being captivated by fear at times, having nightmares and both audio and visual hallucinations of ghost and devils as well as what spiritualist refer to as out of body experiences at the age of five. There was a scary television series that came on at night that my parents watched called The Night Gallery. I would sneak down the stairs and watch it from around the corner with Damon. After being exposed to fear and darkness they fueled my nightmares and became my enemy. I always thought something was out to get me and the fear could come on at any time like a chilling wind forecasting doom. I bought my dad a cool looking skull bank for his birthday when I was a kid. I had nightmares of it chasing me down the hall and after that I hid it nearly every day because I was terrified of it.

I had nightmares about my ventriloquist dummy coming to life and killing me so I locked it in the closet at night. I slept with an arsenal of stuffed animals to protect me at night while I hid under the sheets until I was nearly thirteen years old. Even a simple walk through the woods could end in terror if I let my imagination take over. Remember the Creamoltion cough syrup for children add on TV where the spooky trees chased the kids through the forest? That commercial messed me up big time. It seemed like whatever data was input would be the subject matter of my delusions either positive or negative.

By this age I had also suffered two brain Concussions and been hospitalized on numerous occasions. The first, a head injury from a fall. I was playing with Damon and he dared me to climb up high on a platform at my dad's construction sight where he was playing, It's never the fall that hurts it's the landing. The second head injury was from getting run over by a motorcycle that my brother Damon was riding. He was racing my brother Robert and his friend Bobby Carter while I was standing on the roadside watching and cheering them on. As the racers past on their mini bikes Damon lost control and wiped me out, Bobby gave me mouth to mouth and revived me then I retained consciousness in the hospital hours later screaming in terror.

The very day that I was released from the hospital after the motorcycle accident my parents took us to the best restaurant in our town called Western Travelers where we had fried shrimp. I always loved the Western Travelers because they had a water wheel and a stream inside the restaurant with stuffed raccoons playing in the water. That was cool. After the meal my folks were standing in the parking lot talking to friends, When Damon challenged me and our friend Buddy to a race. I was running across the parking lot with my brother Damon when we fell into a freshly poured parking lot slab of terrazzo concrete that got in my eyes and blinded me. Back to Texas Children's again were they removed my eyes from my head to flush out the crushed glass and cement from my eye sockets. If it had taken my dad any longer to get me to the hospital, a rout he knew well by now, I would have been permanently blind. I was blind for approximately six months while the new eye tissue grew into place. Damon had a field day with this, leading me into walls, moving furniture around and hiding things from me. I do remember that my Aunt Emma Lu gave me a toy gun with a light in it and I would run the batteries down just holding it next to the bandages where I could see its dim red light. It was the only comfort in my darkness and Damon would hide it from me on a daily basis just to be cruel. After my eyes got better and I could see again, I was in my father's electric motor repair shop playing barefoot one night when Damon shut off the lights and ran off leaving me in there alone," on purpose ". Well I ran for the door in terror and stepped on a broken bottle that had fallen during my attempted escape and was now on my way back to the hospital getting my foot sewn back together. Eighteen stitches in my foot and I still have the scar today.

It was a very difficult first five years of child hood with many trips to the hospital. One day Damon and my cousins even made a bomb out of gasoline, clay and a wick. I was running across the yard trying to get away from him when he threw it and set me on fire. Hey the bomb really worked.

Fortunately I had been playing in the woods and I had on me fathers leather hunting vest. It saved my life. I only received first and second degree burns on my arms and legs. Damon got in trouble for playing with gasoline and fire and I got in trouble for wearing my dad's new hunting vest without permission and getting it messed up, go figure that. We had a pet alligator named Allie that Damon had caught. Allie lived in our bath tub until mom told us we couldn't keep it. One day when I came home from school Damon had crucified the baby alligator with sixteen penny nails on a tree in the back yard to watch it die. I was pretty devastated by the ordeal.

CHAPTER FOUR
JESUS AND THE FIRE TRUCK

My parents never went to church. My mother had been forced to go by her dad and my dad had many colorful things to say about the church and preachers, and claimed to have a special deal with God. They still both professed to believe in Christianity and God just like most people in the US that don't want to be persecuted or pestered for non belief. After all this was Texas, Jesus the KKK and pecan pie. Who wouldn't believe that?

The only real live parade I had ever seen on my street was for the vacation bible school at the First Baptist Church of Sheldon and man I wanted to be a part of that. They had clowns and rode on fire trucks, threw candy and knew Jesus personally, who wouldn't want to be a part of that. I would go to church with my next door neighbors the Tollar family. They were Yankees from Wisconsin and Mrs. Tollar played the organ in the church. I remember when I was attending Sunday school, the concepts and subject matter of Christian doctrine where so surreal to me. Jesus on the cross, Jonah in a whale, Daniel with the lions, people hearing voices and seeing visions and most of all, The Devil and his demons.

Even at this young age I was experiencing grandiose delusions of spiritual callings and divine purpose and believed that Satan was trying to kill me because I was chosen by God for a special purpose and that my brother Damon was possessed by the Devil.

I have found time and time again in the church that if you possess any kind of special talent , ability or charisma Christians think that God has created you for his will and purpose and they promote delusions of grandeur to anyone with abilities out of the ordinary especially if they can use you to their advantage.

CHAPTER FIVE
INTRODUCTION TO PLANET SCHOOL

At five years old I entered into public school and came into contact with people outside of my family or church for the first time. It was a fascinating new world to me and I began to excel. After only a short while in school I was given a mental aptitude test and scored with the intelligence of an average ten year old at age five. I needed to be taught the basics like any other child but my ability to think and reason or just plain figure things out on my own was far superior to other children. After the testing was completed I was selected to be a charter student in the first magnet school program in Houston for gifted and talented students. My father who has a great many issues of his own thought that this was some kind of conspiracy and told the school " You're not bussing my kid to some Nigger school in Houston! " it's possible that he thought that this was a program for inter racial busing and did not understand what the program was about. Or maybe he thought it was a special ed program like they had requested for Damon and he was sheltering us and didn't want to admit that his kids were different or had anything wrong with them. He still won't today. Regardless I didn't get to go and I missed the greatest opportunity of my educational life. I think that had I went into the program that not only would caring professionals have nurtured my many talents and abilities but that someone would have diagnosed my illness in it's early stages and I would not be mentally disabled today nor would I have been sucked into religion or drugs, but you never can tell can you. The teachers told my parents that they could not provide the kind of attention that I needed and that they were afraid that I would get bored if I stayed in public school and shut down. They were right, by the third grade I had stopped doing class work or participating in class, I passed everything by having high test scores.

I wasn't a discipline problem until the fifth Grade but I saw school as illogical. All that I saw were a bunch of glorified housewives reciting information out of text books that already had answers in them and that any trained monkey could do the same and that school was a waist of my time and that I had a greater purpose to fulfill than being a cog in the wheel of society.

I really believed that I belonged in a think tank somewhere being raised by scientist and solving problems and writing text books for teachers, not on the other end of the food chain. All it took was one unmotivated old hag named Mrs. Maxwell in the fourth grade to make me stop participating in class all together.

To educators like Mrs. Maxwell: "If you don't like teaching or children you should get another job instead of ruining the educational experience for others."

The power struggles began and I loved the attention. It was really as if my child development was on high speed and that I was experiencing adolescent rebellion in my grade school years. In fact I could easily say that I have been about ten years ahead of my peers in every phase of life. For instance I had already conquered eight years of drugs and alcohol as well as ended a very emotional four year sexual relationship and was a veteran performing artist with many trade skills at the time that most kids were smoking their first joint or just graduating high school. It blew me away when I would see someone make it all the way to college clean and then blow it on Drugs or alcohol as soon as they were on their own for the first time.

I had started experimenting with drugs in Junior high partied through high school " well the ninth grade twice" got a GED and was clean and sober by time for college. What dumb asses. What a waist.

In the sixth grade I failed my first class, it was English of all things and it was my favorite teacher Mrs. Miller. Hell I didn't care, my parents were pre occupied with Damon who had already been thrown out of school by this time and was constantly getting in trouble with the law. It didn't seem to matter whether I did school work or not. I just stopped bringing home report cards and after a while they stopped asking for them. I met my girlfriend when she was in the sixth grade so I failed a year of school on purpose just so I could stay with her another year before we went to high school. I failed another year and they moved me up anyway because I was such a disruption to the other students.

I went to the nurse and counselors office regularly during Jr. High and I explained to them in great detail what was going on in my mind and that I had been having thoughts of suicide and issues, but I was never referred to a doctor or psychiatrist and in fact I was told that I had an attitude problem. I even wrote a story about what I was going through and the difficulties of being a teenager that won fourth place in The Houston Post state wide writing composition contest. Everybody read the story and no one really understood what I was trying to say. I was never entered into a special education program for mental illness because in Texas everything is based on exams and test scores and not only could I pass any exam I had an IQ of one hundred forty at thirteen and I had not participated in class since the third grade.

School was a joke.

Gi
Ki
Th
N

CHAPTER SIX
SEX, DRUGS AND ROCK-N-ROLL

By the sixth grade I was experimenting with different personalities and trying to establish what I was going to be. I was in band because I loved music and I wanted to be a musician so it seemed necessary to learn music. But not being a jock and not fitting in with the band geeks I had to establish myself socially. Being a red neck was too easy in Texas so I established Rock-n-Roll music as the voice of my personality and I just didn't listen to it I lived it. I believed in the Ramones and Rock-n-Roll High school and I wanted to blow up my school too.

I saw my first rock concert at thirteen. It was The Fabulous Thunderbirds, ZZ Top and the Rolling Stones in the Houston Astrodome, What a life changing experience.

Between the ages of thirteen and fifteen I had made the progression from all my classic rock studies of the Beatles, Stones, Yard birds, Hendrix, Doors, and Led Zep, all the way through southern rock ZZ Top, Outlaws, Skynard, Molly Hatchet, Through punk rock with Sex Pistols, Ramones and The Clash, New wave with The Cars, Blondie, The Smiths, Ministry, Depeche Mode, and graduated to Heavy Metal and blues. I stole every book the library had on rock music or guitars and my room was one continuous poster.

The only close I owned were torn up blue jeans and T shirts of rock bands. I was a child prodigy and could play any song that I heard on guitar, bass or drums and

I was playing Iron Maiden, scorpions and Judas Priest in the eighth grade. I just understood music and I could feel it.

I listened to records every day and read rock magazines, emulating the dress and lifestyle portrayed by my Idols who I really considered peers that had gone before me. The most powerful people in the world were Rock stars and this was going to be my chosen profession and I needed to stop wasting my time in school and get on with my destiny. I loved Rock-n-Roll music and it has remained the voice of my people or tribe. As a teen punk rock and heavy metal were passionate vocal and expressive forms of art and a live rock concert was a surrealistic emotional and spiritual high.

A gathering of my people rejected by society and unified by rock-n-roll. Music is power and I understood the power of music.

I was introduced to marijuana at the age of thirteen. I had held off the temptation for several years, My brother smoked pot, my cousins smoked pot and were drug dealers, and one by one my peers started smoking. First Andy, then Thad, then Larry all in about a two week period. One night I spent the night with my friend Jimmy who had stole some pot from his mom. We both lied to each other about smoking before but soon confessed to each other when we were lying on the floor laughing our ass off and stoned for the first time. Boy did things change after that. By the end of that month I had tried marijuana, hashish, opium and mandrax and I had seen someone overdose on intravenous drugs. Not to mention that Thad's folks Ella and Jerry, who were like my second parents owned a liquor store and grandma Parker would let us sneak a bottle of whatever we wanted when we helped her stock the shelves. We wanted to be rock stars so we lived like one. I even dropped my first hit of acid in the seventh grade at the Rocky Horror Picture Show. Not only did this completely fuck up my since of sexuality but I was French kissed by a hot girl with a Mohawk that I didn't know while I was tripping my balls off and watching the movie. Kind of hard to go back to cheerleaders after that. I met that girl again about four years later and she remembered me, after that we were partners hanging out in Montrose for about six months. She's dead now; I think she died of aids.

I had stopped attending church because of the prejudices that now applied towards me. I had been unknowingly self medicating as a means to stabilize my illness and since everything I believed was wrong according to the church including Rock music, "I was a musician and loved rock music" girls "I had a beautiful girlfriend that I was already having sex with and wasn't about to stop for Jesus" and smoking pot "which was the only thing that calmed me down or made me feel half way normal". For the next eight years I devoted my energies toward using my special powers or gifts to become a rock star and hating Christians. If God wouldn't love me because I was different then I was going to play for the other side. From the age of thirteen until I was twenty I smoked marijuana, and experimented with Cocaine, LSD, Opium, Hashish, Mandrax, mushrooms, Quaaludes, Rjs, Rj8's, Ecstasy , Crystal Meth and I was a teenage alcoholic. I worked to make money to buy equipment (drugs were almost always free when your popular and in a band),

I partied to increase my popularity and fame and I wrote music and played in bands. Everything that I did was geared towards fulfilling my destiny. I knew that if I worked hard enough that I would be an international Rock Star by the age of nineteen and this was my only goal.

CAPTER SEVEN
THE GIRL OF MY DREAMS AND
THE WOMAN OF MY NIGHTMARES

I had met my only girlfriend Athea when I was thirteen and in the eighth grade. I can still remember clearly the first time that I ever saw her beautiful face. She was the only girl that I ever dated or slept with and I considered her my wife, she was my soul mate and I intended to be with her forever. She is still today the most beautiful and special woman that I have ever known and my life is incomplete without her. Athea and her two sisters Cheri and Terra lived with their aunt Peggy and uncle Mike who owned a bar called Heartbreakers. Every day I would ride the school bus to Athea's house and stay there until her folks got home and then walk to Thad's or walk the full five miles home.

On weekends I would ride my bike and we would meet in the park. Where we would hold each other for hours and dream of the day that we could be together forever.

She was my girl and I was her man.

When I was sixteen years old my parents left Houston and moved to Austin, TX, I quit school so I could return to Houston to see Athea and jam with my friends. One weekend while jamming with my friend Mike English, we were discovered by a rock music producer and were invited into the studio to do some recording for a demo. We were hardly sixteen and could play dueling lead guitar solos. The very next day I was on my way to get some fresh guitar strings when Mike and I had a motorcycle accident and were laid up for six months. A woman driving a delivery truck pulled out in front of us and just stopped. I broke my left arm, left leg and crushed my left ankle. Mike who was on the back of the bike flew completely over the truck that we hit and landed on the other side sustaining only minor injuries bruised kidneys and ripped ligaments in his knees.

It was during the time of my recovery that Athea left me and ran off to New York with another man. He was a man much older than me and she married him to get away from her mother and her home life. His name was Jerry and he was abusive and unfaithful to her and treated her like shit but she was his girl now.

I was devastated! I could not understand it. I truly loved her and thought we were meant to be together forever. At seventeen years old I was completely suicidal and I suffered my first nervous or psychotic breakdown. Life basically meant nothing at all to me and this fueled my hatred towards God even more. I never dated another girl and I hated women from that time on.

CHAPTER EIGHT
SATAN'S PLAN REVIELED

Now I was living in Austin, the live music capital of the world and I had moved my friends Mike and Jimmy from Houston and teamed up with a bass player from Florida named Art Napoli and started a band called Texas Metal. Music was going through some changes at that time and we were playing everything from Metallica to Iron Maiden and from Rush to Megadeth as well as our own brand of hate fueled rebellious music. I felt as if I were trapped in Austin, until I met Art, we had a common vision and addiction and Art wanted to be a rock star too. I talked him into quitting school to practice every day and we played at our first Live Music festival called Wood Shock at seventeen years old with our band Texas Metal force. **

I convinced my childhood friends Jimmy and Mike to leave home and join Art and I in our effort to take over the world. During this period of time we partied like rock stars. I played with this band and its consecutive offspring bands until I was kicked out of my own band for being too controlling and too wasted all the time.
It was like going through a divorce, I loved these guys and they just could not understand my drive and ambition and all rock stars were wasted, it was a prerequisite. At the age of nineteen I returned to Houston to work in the petrochemical industry and to put myself through music school.
By the time I reached the age of twenty I was living in a warehouse studio loft in Houston, still attending music school, teaching private guitar lessons and partying on the weekends.
One week end I went to an outdoor rock concert that I had seen advertised at the

local liquor store. At the concert there were three friends of mine from school that had become born again Christians and had a Christian metal band. When I went backstage to visit them this evangelical guy named Chris Jenkins from a similar heavy metal background was trying to convince me that Satan had possessed my mind and body through heavy metal music and that the voices in my head were demons. I told him he was full of shit, that's when I had my first full blown audio hallucination where I heard the voice of God tell me that "I was un pure and that I was arguing with a child of God".

Well being completely freaked out by this experience I of course repented and joined a church the next day. When I explained to the pastors and clergy the background I had come from and that even though I had accepted Jesus and believed, I was still hearing the voices and the voices told me that Jesus wasn't real, They all jumped on me and started performing an exorcism and casting the demons out of me right there on the stage in front of everyone. They said that the reason the demons had such a strong hold on me was because of the special calling on my life and that I would need the help of the holy spirit to give me power over the demons, then gave me bible scriptures to back up all crap they were telling me. I bought it all hook line and sinker.

Well not wanting to be a pawn of Satan anymore and needing an answer for my talents, insight, abilities and obsessive drive as well as seeing visions and hearing voices, after all I had been in heavy metal bands and listened to Satanic heavy metal music, I had been wasted and hated Christians for eight years, so it was completely logical to believe that I was possessed by Satan. After all it was in the bible.

I received the gift of the holy spirit with the evidence of speaking in tongues (babbling a bunch of psychotic bullshit that doesn't mean anything) and was completely delivered from eight years drugs and alcohol. I not only believed that I had been tricked into serving Satan and doing his will, but that the feelings I had for Athea were born in sin and that the only reason that I wanted her was because she was the embodiment of beauty and carnal sin. So I stopped listening to all secular music and married the first Christian girl I met that was the complete opposite of Athea in every way. I married a nineteen year old former bar maid named Cindy with a four year old daughter named Danielle. I was happy and life was good for the next five years. Cindy and I had two children together Aaron and Natolie. Well with this new power, I found that through prayer and meditation in the scriptures and by babbling in tongues for hours I could occupy my mind and control the voices in my head or at least discern between the voice of God, the voice of the Spirit, my own mind and the voice of Satan. Now I had all the answers, I had super powers beyond that of mere mortals and I had become the Apostle Nathon Dees. During this time I was involved in a petrochemical plant explosion at work and received second and third degree burns on one fourth of my body including my face arm and chest. Since I had been delivered from drugs by Jesus I had to take a stand and make a testimony out of my life for other believers.

I refused to take any pain medication and I went through a month of de breeding and skin removal with no pain killer at all just praying and chanting in tongues while they exposed my nerve endings so new skin could grow. I had the powers of a shaman and could even control physical pain through my beliefs.

Woodshock

IN PROCESS

Woodshock 83'
By Mike Alvarez

Woodshock 83'

To get to the Hurlbut Ranch where Blaine wanted to hold the concert, you would have to drive on the roughest dirt roads you can imagine. In one newspaper article that reviewed the first show, the writer described the drive to the ranch as "driving down stairs" – and that was about right. On my first drive to the ranch, I thought "no way". The car would bottom out, get stuck in deep ridges in the road – a nightmare. But when we hit the clearing and saw the ranch – it was a beautiful sight. Furthermore, there were the water holes. There were two water holes, "Deadman's" and another smaller private hole that only the Hurlbut family used. It was a picture out of Heaven. I obviously didn't care how many people would show up to a show there. Those that would come - would never forget it.

I recruited Charles Gunning ("Doug The Slug") to help put a show together.   He was a feared thug and club bouncer at the time – everyone was pretty much afraid of him. He had a thing for Lisa Gamache, my band mate (Max and the Makeups lead singer), so he was always around us and I took a liking to him. He was working at Dan's Liquor at the time and managed to borrow a giant truck from the store.   We planned to use the truck to store musical gear during the show and we used it to move things out to the sight. The truck sort of gave us a look of organization though we were far from organized.   Before I would agree to do a show there, I had Blaine take Doug and I through all of the caves, jump off all of the cliffs and danger spots as I knew the punks would try anything if it was there to try.

I think Jeff Smith got interested early, bringing some San
Antonio bands, including his band Bang Gang, and a lot
of the local hard core punk bands to our attention. Local
musician and professional sound man Johnny Medina agreed
to bring his sound system to the event and he did so for five years. The festival would become the world's
premiere alternative
music festival for its time between 1983 & 1987.   The
lineup for the first show in the hills would include Max
and The Makeups, The Jitters, Crotch Rot, The Offenders,
Channel 3, The Ideals, Skank, New Torpedoes, Human
Drama, Bang Gang, Tiger Roos, Texas Metal Force and Pleasure Method.

Texas Metal Force/ Woodshock

Nathon Dees and Art Napoli

CHAPTER NINE
THE HOUSE OF CARDS COLLAPSES

How could I possibly be wrong? I made straight A's in seminary, I was a brilliant orator, I was successful, talented and people believed in me because I was called, set apart, recognized by my peers, licensed and ordained to preach the gospel, heal the sick, cast out demons, lead people to the kingdom of God and operate in the gifts of the spirit. I was completely delusional totally schizoaffective and on my way to the funny farm. I existed this way for nearly fifteen years before I was finally diagnosed as being mentally ill and woke up from the fairy tale land of Christianity. During this time I studied the bible day and night, went to devotionals, attended church every time the doors were open, stayed with the elders of the church performing exorcisms and casting out demons from people and holding independent bible studies in my home. When I wasn't doing this I was playing in an evangelical Christian rock band called Antidote and doing street ministry. My only purpose in life was to let people know about Jesus and deliver folks from hell.

This went on for five years before my first wife Cynthia backslid and went back into the world of alcoholism and partying. When Cindy left home I knew that it was time to file for a divorce. I didn't believe in divorce but I felt I had no option. If Cindy was going to turn her back on God she was an infidel. I was sure that I would get custody of Aaron and Natolie our two children and that I would get the house because I had the Kids. There was no way that I could possibly lose, I was in ministry, I was clean and sober, I was an outstanding member of the church, a Free Mason, a business owner, and there was no way that I could lose in divorce court to a drunk and a whore that abandoned her children. I was wrong, I lost everything. I lost custody of my two children because I had a dick. I lost my brand new house that I had built myself and paid cash for because I did not have custody of the kids and I lost my faith because the only comfort that was offered to me by my pastor was "consider Job "a popular bible character that lost everything in a game between God and Satan to prove Job's loyalty to God. This sucked.

To make things worse the day that I was forced to leave my home and give up my children I asked God why this had to happen and he spoke to me audibly (another hallucination) and told me " It was not his will for me to be with Cindy but that in two years I would marry Athea". Well this made me furious with God. If I was meant to be with Athea then why did I have to endure this suffering and have my children with the wrong woman?

I knew that drugs and alcohol weren't the answer, I couldn't go back to the church. It was at this time that my old party buddy Bobby Daniels heard about what happened to me and felt like it was his duty to show me a good time. After five years of being clean and sober it only took one invitation to party from Bobby and I was out on the dance floor every week end wigging on X and completely free from God and Cindy and making plans to start a punk rock cult following.

The Christian Rock band Antidote

Nathon Dees, Chris Valenti, and Grady Myers

Chapter Ten
A Way Out

I felt like I was out of control and needed to be institutionalized. I knew I would die from drug abuse if I started a band and I had no personal strength without Christ.

I needed a way to regroup and start over, I knew that if I didn't pull my shit together I would never receive custody of my children so at twenty five years old I enlisted in the US Army. I actually had to fight to get in the Army. I was a divorced twenty five year old white male with a GED and they didn't want me.

It was a great plan, in the Army I could pay my child support, get away from Cindy and I wouldn't need to worry about food or clothing, plus with a three year enlistment it was impossible for God's will to take effect concerning Athea because I was obligated to the government for a minimum of three years and I could stay away from drugs there. The first Day that I was in basic training I was pulled aside by a Pentecostal drill sergeant that had read my personnel file. He told me that I was there because God had a special plan for my life and that although I was mad at God he still loved me and had a special purpose for me. How could God find me here, I was running away from him. I got a job killing people so I could die in combat and make my children proud and my X wife suffer not so I could serve God. During this time I was completely manic, working with the chaplains corps and attending

Pentecostal church on Sunday and playing soldier while getting drunk every other night. I excelled in the Army earning two field grade promotions and four Army achievement awards in less than two years. I was on fire, I had a purpose again and I was institutionalized where all I had to do was meet or exceed a set standard and I would be recognized and rewarded.

During my stay at Fort Sill I had decided at one point that if I defaced my body that God would reject me from the calling and I would be free. At first I just pierced my nipple and my nose but not wanting to be a poser I soon committed to tattooing my skin which was a major sin. That's when I met my friend Rocky, he was a Christian biker tattoo artist that was a former president of the Vietnam Vets motorcycle club. Rocky told me the same thing that everyone else did, I was special and God had a plan for me and that right now I was just pissed off at God. Rocky taught me that I could be a Christian without being a dick. Meeting someone that I could respect from my world that was a Christian helped perpetuate my faith during my time of spiritual darkness.

After only "you guessed it" two years in the Army I woke up one morning expecting to hear from God, so I sat down and meditated with a pen and paper waiting to hear from God and I did. The audible voice of God spoke to me and told me that my time of isolation and rebuilding was over and that I was leaving the Army but not to worry about where I would go or what I would do because he was in complete control and that his will would be done in my life. The very next day my captain called me into his office and told me that I had lost my security clearance because the Army had found out that I had filed bank bankruptcy before enlisting in the Army and that I could reenlist with a new non secure MOS or that I could go home with a full honorable discharge and all my benefits.

I consulted with all my superiors and they all said the same thing. "PFC Dees you came here a broken man now you've rebuilt yourself, go home and start over because you can do anything you want and you're wasting your time here". Well that's not the speech I was expecting at all, but it was the truth so I left Fort Sill and went back to Austin to write and record a new album and start a band.

CHAPTER ELEVEN
BACK TO THE WITCHDOCTORS

While I was recording the album I would have periods of confusion where I could not think or concentrate because of the flood of thoughts going through my head, then I heard the word reprobate in my mind and remembered the scripture that said a double minded man was unstable in all his ways and would be given over to a reprobate mind. I thought that I was losing my mind and that I would go insane if I did not serve God. I made an appointment to see a pastor friend in Houston that was into demonic deliverance ministry and left Austin the next day.

When I got to Houston I had some time to kill so I went to my kids' school to meet their teachers and see how they were doing, that's when I found out that since the time that I left for the Army my X wife Cindy had gone completely out of control and that both of my children were being physically abused and neglected by their mother and that I had better make preparations to take custody of my children. Well I knew that Cindy and I didn't see eye to eye but I had no Idea that she had become a severe child abuser while I was in the Army. Well by this time I was pretty shook up by the whole ordeal and went on to my appointment with Brother Robert Pitts the Christian prophet to find out what was really happening to me. When I arrived at his house he was ready for me and told me that God had told him that I was coming and prepared him for the meeting. When I explained to him what was going on in my head and with my life, (basically explaining to him the symptoms of Schizoaffective disorder) he proceeded to explain how that I had allowed Satan to have a toe hold in my life through my rebellion towards God and how that I would need to go through complete demonic deliverance no matter what it took. After he called all the prayer warriors in the church he then called another pastor friend of his to join us and we drove to the church where they took me to their upper prayer room and started the exorcism. After repenting and renouncing and denouncing Satan and everything you could imagine these guys laid hands on me and blabbed in tongues and screamed at demons until my brain shorted out and I fell to the floor.

 My third nervous or psychotic breakdown. Well hell after that I didn't hear any voices and if I did I surely wasn't going to tell these guys.

CHAPTER TWELVE
ATHEA AND THE SUPER CHURCH

Well now that I was cleansed and pure again I sure didn't want to get to far from the church and I needed to come up with a plan to fight for the custody of my children. I had one more thing that I needed to do, find Athea and tell her I was sorry for hating her for so long and that I forgave her.

I figured that I would go to her parents bar and see where I could find her.

I drove to her town and went to find her. I found her Aunt Peggy and told her I wanted to see Athea, she told me that Athea never came there anymore because she was a born again Christian and that if I wanted to see her I needed to go to The Abundant Life Christian Center in La Marque, TX so I visited the Wednesday night service hoping to see Athea who I had not seen in ten years.

This was a giant super church televised worldwide, there were thousands of people there and I didn't think I would find her there so I enjoyed the service and figured that God had some other reason for me to be there.

When the service was over I walked down the corridor on my way out disappointed not to see her, but glad I came; when there she was. It was the girl of my dreams standing there in a church, saved, born again, single and more beautiful than I could have ever imagined. This was the first time that I had seen Athea as an adult woman. I had always convinced myself that Athea's looks would deteriorate rapidly from the hard living and not to expect that much, after all she had two kids. I was wrong! She was absolutely exquisite. From her beautiful long hair cascading gently over her shoulders to her tall, slim perfectly molded body filling her mid length black dress. Her face was the face a girl I once knew sculpted into the Image of a Greek Goddess. She was once again the most beautiful woman that I had ever seen.

That night we went for coffee with her sister Cheri that had also been born again and I told them my saga and what I had been through that week. Cheri had just graduated from seminary at Abundant Life and Athea was enrolled for the next semester. The next day I returned to

Austin packed up my goods and moved back to Houston were I took a job with room and board and enrolled myself in seminary.

I needed to be closer to my children so I could help them and so I could start developing a case against my X wife and eventually win custody of my children. I wanted to be closer to Brother Robert because he had helped deliver me from Satan so I apprenticed under him while I went to school with Athea. I was holding on to the promise that God have gave me that I would marry Athea in two years but I never told her what I believed, in addition Bro. Robert told me that God had spoke to him and that Athea and I would be wed.

We never dated, I never asked her out and all we did was go to church, study and let our children play together when I had weekend visitations with Aaron and Natolie.

"Out of everything that I have ever experienced in spiritualism I can now explain it through psychology and credit to my mental illness, all of the voices, all of the visions, the highs and the lows, the beliefs, everything; but there is one event that I will never be able to explain"

One night while attending seminary Athea and I were doing homework together and listening to Christian music and talking. I told Athea just in conversation that If I had a wife I would like to learn ball room dancing because I thought it would be cool to do something like that with your girl. She told that she had made an impossible list for God, one that no man could fulfill and that over the course of time that we had been together God had shown her one by one that I fulfilled everything on that list and that ballroom dancing was the last thing on the list.

I asked her to dance and this was the first time I had held her close or touched her in any intimate way since we had reunited. When I held her in my arms and started dancing I immediately felt my very being leave my body and enter into hers, go completely through her and return back into my body. At that very moment Athea pulled away from me startled and asked what just happened. She explained to me that at that instant she could not tell the difference between she and I, and she knew beyond any doubt that she was holding her husband. We were married on December 16, 1996 and with her two young sons Teagan and Haeden with us we started a new life and began building a child custody case to win the battle for Aaron and Natolie so our household could be complete. Just as a side note, at some point between the end of this chapter and the beginning of the next I was building custom cedar chest in my woodworking shop when a board got sucked into my table saw and I cut off the finger tips on my left hand. I actually heard the voice of God tell me to pick up my push board and I replied back " I'm Nathon Dees Master Craftsman" , "I can handle this" as the board sucked into the blade. I pushed the bloody nubs together and wrapped up my hand and packed it in ice and my brother Robert took my to three different hospitals until he found a surgeon that could sew them back on. Thanks Rob!

For years I had struggled with my pride being a musician, well that was over now. If I could ever even play again I would be happy. I remember Art telling me that the curse was broken and I was free from being a musician and could live a normal life now. It took me years to retrain myself to play and the fingers were never quite the same but I retained my virtuosity.

Nathon, Athea, Aaron, Natolie, Headen and Teagan.

CHAPTER THIRTEEN
TAKING OVER THE WORLD

Athea and I both had issues to work out but as long as we had Jesus we would find a way. I was working as an associate pastor at Bro. Roberts' church and studying family law over the internet. Athea and I were living in the parsonage of the church and involved in ministry and our children full time. During this time I also had a vision from God " which pastors do" and I converted the youth department of the church and the gym which wasn't being used into the largest Christian teen club and espresso bar in the city of Houston, with live music every weekend as well as pool, foosball, darts, roller skating and a cool atmosphere for teenagers. I had moved my friends recording studio into the teen club and was on my way to being the one of the most influential people in the Christian rock music scene in Houston. I had bands booked from all over the state. After only a few months of operation there were more people visiting The Café Esprit "which I had named the club" than there were people attending church on Sunday. This would not do. The Church soon complained that the families coming on Friday and Saturday nights didn't attend our church but were from other churches and that some of the kids that were coming weren't Christians.
"NO DUUH, THAT WAS THE POINT DUMBASSES!"
The problem of my life, if you accomplish more than your superiors and it makes them look bad and you lose favor quickly. The Café Esprit ministry was taken away from me and given to someone else to run after accusations were made accusing me of having my own crazy agenda "like saving the lost" and I was forced to resign. All I could see was a lack of vision and complacency. If these people really believed in God, than nothing would be more important than reaching people for Christ and no vision was too big for God. The Café Esprit is still in operation today but it never fully accomplished what I had set out for it to do.
By this time I had filed for the child custody case Pro Se and Athea and I did all the case research ourselves. When I had finished doing my homework I had over 500 pages of reports from child protective services on abuse and neglect towards my children and eighteen police reports for domestic disturbances at my X wife's house. Aaron

was in the third grade at this time and was sleeping in class and had a fifty percent grade average in school and was failing every subject. He was too intelligent to get a learning disability label and was labeled as having an emotional disorder. Athea tutored Aaron on Wednesday nights and weekends and brought him up to a B average in one semester and he passed the year on high test scores. I could see a carbon copy of myself in Aaron, only compounded by the fact that he had been physically abused by his mother and was involved in an ugly custody battle. We even found out that while I was in the service Cindy would leave the children at home alone for days at a time and that Aaron who was nine was caring for Natolie who was five. When Athea and I took the case to trial the evidence that we presented was so strong that we were given soul managing conservatorship of the children and Athea was made their legal mother. We also got my house back because Cindy didn't pay the taxes on it. As soon we won custody of the kids we sold the house, packed our bags and moved to Wimberley, Texas were I would design and build a 2400 sq ft house with five bedrooms , two and a half baths, a studio, two car garage and my beautiful wife and our four children. I thought the trouble was finally over and things were going to be easy now. I was making good money sometimes, we were living in our dream home that we built ourselves, Athea was home schooling all four children and running her massage business, while I built houses, put in septic systems, built a motel for my father and I owned

and operated a custom motorcycle shop with my old buddy Art who was still playing in bands and partying. I still had no Idea that I was anything less than anointed and ambitious, driven and motivated with a grand purpose for life as long as I could do enough to keep the forces of Satan from entering into my mind and destroying God's plan for my life. There was nothing that could stop me as long as I could discern the voice of Satan and follow the voice of God". We were as my friend Don Cool would say" Partridge Family Jesus Freaks " serving the Lord ministering to bikers, rehabilitating drug attics in our own home and serving faithfully in a local church, once again playing in the music ministry and doing demonic deliverance ministry on other mentally ill Christians.

CHAPTER FOURTEEN
THE DEVILS BACK IN TOWN

About the time of the 9/11 attack I was having problems with my marriage because Athea who is still a Christian, thought I didn't really love her for some reason. We could speak in tongues, hear the voice of God, see demons and angels how could Athea not know I was in love with her. Well this must have been the greatest Demonic attack of my life because neither God or the Holy Ghost would defend me in this matter and tell my wife the truth that I would have gladly laid down my own life for her. Sometimes I had trouble controlling my emotions but I was always faithful to my marriage and I loved my wife. Athea was the object of my every affection and fulfilled my every romantic fantasy so why would I want someone else?

Her own feelings of inadequacy and concepts of self value and worth which being bi polar and a man I could not possibly understand drove her to believe that no man could truly love his wife or at least I did not love her.

Well when she stopped having sex with me because I didn't love her well that was the straw that broke the camel's back. I was really cracking up over this and the thought of losing everything again when I had done nothing wrong only entered me into the "Holy Job" category again which I did not want to be in.

I was painting olive oil crosses on the doors and windows of the house, I was anointing my head with oil and walking the lengths of my property in the name of Jesus to prevent Satan from lying to my wife and I was slowly losing my mind. I saw demons around every corner and new Satan was destroying me through my wife once again.

The only way that I was able to deal with my intense sex drive was to be married. I was a good provider, a faithful loving and husband and father and was deeply and passionately in love with my wife. To deny me sex on the basis on infidelity was an insult to everything that I was and everything that I believed.

During this time of trouble my good friend Rabbi Bruce Abraham whom I respected a great deal gave me a joint of some really good marijuana and told me I had better smoke it and just chill the fuck out for a while or I was going to lose it for good. Bruce told me that I had lost touch with reality and that my wife was fucked up too.

I have found this to be very sound advice and good council. When I sat down in my back yard and smoked that joint, for the first time since I had been saved on Nov 11,1987, I realized that everything in my life was a complete lie if Athea did not know our love was real after what we had experienced together in the supernatural " the exchange of souls" and that if I truly believed the things I professed to believe as a Christian about demons controlling our thoughts and Satan destroying my marriage than I was a complete paranoid schizophrenic and that I was no different than the religious extremist Muslim kooks that performed the terror acts of 9/11. This was either the most enlightening event of my life or Satan had complete control of my mind. My wife, along with my friends and peers in the church said that this was an attack from Satan or attributed it to the pot but I knew clearly by this time that I had wandered out of my Jesus box and I knew too much to ever go back in.

I'm Really glad to save this pic. This is my 1964 Corvier Hornet Trike from when I owned my bike shop! I sure have had some Good Times!..N8

Hill Country Hawgs Bike Shop. Wimberley, Texas

CHAPTER FIFTEEN
RUN AWAY, RUN FAR AWAY FAST

Jaco, Beach Costa Rica

I needed to find out the truth once and for all so in a classic bi polar move I divorced the girl of my dreams (who didn't believe I loved her any way), closed my business, sold and gave away everything that I had, took my two kids and moved to a beach on the pacific coast of Costa Rica far away from everyone and everything.
Here I would find out once and for all what was real and what was not. During this time period I did a lot of soul searching and inner healing dealing with hating my wife and hating Christians. Still completely delusional undiagnosed and untreated and without religion to protect me from myself I partied my ass off, surfed, swam, played guitar and

tried to come up with a new purpose or plan. I had lots of new non Christian Friends and I got to play music a lot and pot was legal, cheap and plentiful. I wanted to meet someone new but knew that the chances of ever finding someone as wonderful as Athea would be next to impossible and I wasn't about to settle for less.

I decided to open another teen club but this time without interference from the church. I would create a safe place for Costa Rican kids to hang out and teach my new doctrine called " Pull your head out of your ass" which was based on principles of common sense without the use of religious fear and nirvana manipulation to get the point across. I leased a building and completely built out a live music venue with an espresso bar, stage, lights, sound system and a restaurant.

Nathon's Place was completely finished and all I was waiting for was my operating permit. That's when I found out that I had leased a building that had been built illegally and could not be permitted. The guy who owned the building knew there were problems with the city but thought he would have the issues resolved before I found out that he was a liar and a thief and had stole my money. I lost nearly thirty thousand dollars and six months of work.

On top of everything else that could have went wrong, my brother Evil Damon had been released from prison and my father thought he just needed a new start too so he broke Damon's parole and illegally smuggled him into Costa Rica. All he wanted to do "he said" was move far away into the mountains and disappear. It took less than two weeks for him to be a complete lunatic crack head running the streets of my new home town stealing from people and causing trouble. I had once again been sold out by my dad and linked to this blood sucking criminal just because he was my brother. I hated Damon and left the country to get away from this piece of shit in the first place.

After nine months of effort to start a new business and life in Costa Rica everything I had tried fell through for one reason or another and now my brother who I hated and feared was here with me. I soon suffered another nervous breakdown.

CHAPTER SIXTEEN
THE CRASH LANDING BACK HOME

I was broke and hopeless and ready to go home. I had a new explanation and mission when I returned to the US, I was still an apostle, but God had called me out of the church because I had been chosen to bring the light of God to non Christians and stand in direct opposition to the false Christian church and their lying doctrines. I went back to the states and started a nonprofit association and started counseling people in the community with two other pastor friends Mike Klumpp and Steve Townsend that had been excommunicated by the church for not agreeing with mainstream Christian doctrine.

Both Mike and Steve were licensed ministers and counselors. Mike is the author of The Single Dads Survival Guide, a martial arts expert and a biker. Steve is the president of the Alliance Motorcycle ministry, he is the official Chaplin over every outlaw motorcycle club in Central Texas and is on the board of directors of the Confederation of Clubs in Texas.

Mike is the first person that diagnosed me as being Bi Polar one night while we were talking about our clients and then Steven told me that he was Bi Polar too.

During this time I was again completely manic and making all kinds of things happen, I had reunited the children with their mother and was helping to rehabilitate my X wife Cindy, I built a miniature golf course and BMX bike track and opened it free for kids in the community and I was writing and recording an album of anti Christian hate music that God had inspired me to write while I was in Costa Rica.

I was running all of my father's business while he was in Costa Rica dealing with Damon. During this time I was also getting a band together to take the truth of God to my people the bikers, skaters, surfers and rock n rollers the people that had not bought into the lies of Christianity. I was getting ready to take over the world and willing to die for what I believed was true. Then things went sour again.

Cindy started drinking again and Aaron got busted for pot at school and Damon was expelled from Costa Rica For the first of many times. I had all of the influences from society in the US, all the churches and all my Christian friends waiting for me to be delivered from Satan once again and my beautiful wife Athea whom I already had plans to remarry, speaking in tongues and claiming our marriage in the name of Jesus (God finally told her that I really loved her) and praying for me all the time and trying to suck me back into the delusional lies of Christian faith. Well between that, my business, my investments in Costa Rica and my new found anti Christian faith and the return of my fugitive brother. I suffered my final nervous or psychotic break down to date.

That is when I finally put down my theology books and started studying psychology for an answer.

The Outpost Motel, First Motel in Dripping Springs Nathon Dees, Athea Dees, Byron Dees, Hubert L. Roberts

CHAPTER SEVENTEEN
LOOSING MY RELIGION

I had studied the bible for years just learning how to decipher its meanings and languages so I could understand the truth, It only took one week of research for me to completely understand what was happening to me, where it came from and how long it had been effecting my life.

First I went to the book store and bought a book on surviving bi polar disorder since that was my obvious goal. After reading this book and researching RH Factor and schizophrenia on the internet I knew way more than I wanted to know. Next I needed to have a greater understanding of some of the subject matter I was reading so I went to a Goodwill store and bought a med school Psychology book for five dollars took it home and read it from cover to cover. Then I started hitting libraries and researching schizophrenia. It was real, it was proven, it was science and most of all didn't require faith to believe.

I was mentally ill, had been for a long time and I had gone as far as I could go.

Then I went a step farther and got some books that were taboo to the church and I studied philosophy and its origins completely laying out the history of modern thought and the birth of religions and even their purposes. I still wasn't quite sure if I would still need to confront Satan or not so I bought a book called The Exhaustive Encyclopedia of Demonology and witchcraft.

I would carry this book around just to see the fear in people's faces when they asked what you were reading. I had studied Satanism, the occult, witchcraft and pagan religion in the church and new a great deal about the dark side but this book was not what I expected. It was just what it said it was an encyclopedia. A chronological life time study in alphabetical order of the history of Satanism, witchcraft and demonology.

This book made the Foxes Book of Martyrs "required reading for all Christian seminary students" look like a stroll in the park. There was no way to compare what other people did to Christians against what Christians did to other people. When I read what people believed and did throughout the history of Christianity after they created Satan and his demons to manipulate people with fear I understood that I was a part of a nearly two thousand year old lie.

The rituals practiced in the dark ages by Christian witch hunters were the same exact same theories and practices that had been applied to me and that I had applied to others. The arts of exorcism and demonic deliverance were developed during this 1800 year old Christian practice of hunting down and killing witches. The text that the church used to establish the doctrines of the dark crafts where written by men that were writing instructions for the persecution of anyone practicing the dark crafts and instructions on torturing and killing witches.

The rest of the doctrine was established by the testimony of the innocent people that confessed under severe torture and were murdered any way. Being one of the few Christians eaten by lions would have been a pick-nick compared to what open courts sanctioned and ruled by the church did to millions of men women and children in the name of Jesus.

I had become so delusional as a Christian that I was performing mid evil psychology on myself my family and my friends. I was using the same lame pathetic unrealistic theories that these assholes in the book used to kill people from about two hundred AD until the witch hunts of Salem. Satanism was created by Christianity and the two had to co exist. Christianity is a fear/reward based doctrine designed to manipulate the simple and the mentally ill. It's all inclusive unless you're a fag or you're just not stupid enough to believe it. I thought Satan was out to kill me because the bible said so and the bible was true.

I believed in demons because they were in the bible. I thought psychology was the enemy of god because it said that normal people prayed and even had faith but only mentally ill people are able to hear or see metaphysical beings. The bible says if you can't hear my voice you must not know me.

Hell everyone in the bible hears voices and sees metaphysical beings and we all know that God's word is forever and never changes so it must be true for today.

Well Mr. Bi Polar book and the DSM-IV says that if you hear voices it is a symptom of mental illness and this book isn't two thousand years old, it's cutting edge medical technology covering years of scientific research and data. This book says if you see visions, you are hallucinating and you should try some Risperdone. The bible talked about transcendence and out of body experiences. Well so did the psychology book and by the time that I understood the depth of schizophrenia I was glad just to be Schizoaffective. I had all the symptoms of severe juvenile onset Chronic rapid cycling Bi Polar one disorder and young adult schizophrenia with mixed episodes and I had them for a long, long time.

I could have never been properly diagnosed as long as I was a Christian because I would have even considered the questioning during the diagnoses as being anti Christian and trying to devalue my beliefs. Only unbelievers didn't believe what the bible said and I did see devils and angels, and I could hear the voice of God.

I was the Rev, Nathon Q, Dees and the only way that I could accept something that was actually going to destroy my very identity, I was going to need to be born again, again.

This time born of the flesh not of the spirit and grounded in secular reasoning. No metaphysics, if it's not physical don't take it for granted that it is real or that it's even there. No concepts of an afterlife but a greater understanding of life itself. No more alternate realities, the most real fact I could understand was that I was severely mentally ill and I had eluded treatment by entering into a fantasy world where my symptoms were perfectly normal, totally acceptable and even admired and encouraged. In fact my life has now become completely useless because I have lost the ability to believe and dream. I don't want to get sucked into another cult or a messed up relationship just because I want to achieve the delusion of being happy when happiness itself is only a concept derived from teachings, experiences and beliefs.

CHAPTER EIGHTEEN
IS SIGMOND IN THE HOUSE?

By the time I finished my research I knew for a fact that I was mentally ill and had been the whole time. This was the third time I had went to a doctor for mental and emotional issues but it was the first time that I had educated myself enough to know that science was not the enemy of God and was prepared to accept the diagnoses. Since I had diagnosed myself and I had done a tremendous amount of research on the science of mental illness I was looking for a confirmation and boy did I get one.

Three different mental health professionals concluded that I did in fact have extreme Schizoaffective disorder and that my sixteen year old son had it too. One doctor said that it was unbelievable that I had never been hospitalized for my condition and wanted to know how that I could have possibly survived so long without medical treatment. "The answer was easy" I told him, I was a right wing charismatic Christian and in fact a pastor involved in demonic deliverance ministry and that all of my hallucinations both audible and visual as well as my emotional problems and mania were perfectly acceptable in Christian doctrine and better yet even validated the gifts of my calling. I had been institutionalized with a lot of other mentally ill people using mid evil psychiatry to explain away our mental and emotional problems and the largest support group of idiots in the world to back me up and a bible to prove it. Then I was institutionalized in the Army were all I had to do was follow orders and be extreme which I was good at, they told me everything I needed to know. I knew what to wear, when to eat, what to say and had a complete itinerary of things to do each day.

Finally I had been institutionalized in marriage, as long as I could bring home a pay check and stay erect I was OK. I had a full time nurse taking care of me as long as I was married. My clothes were washed my children were cared for and I didn't need to worry about sex. It was when Athea and I separated that I realized that I knew what I was supposed to do but I just couldn't do it. I was afraid of money and as long as someone else paid all of my bills I just needed to focus on making more money.

When I start doing finance, I start devaluing my own existence to the point that I hate very concept of money and wish that I lived in a communal society of craftsmen and farmers that traded goods amongst themselves. Some people like money and some people are good with it, I hate it and I'm either afraid to spend it or I invest it recklessly. Don't get me wrong I know how to make money and I've made lots of it. It is the concepts of value or self worth being attached to a trade or job and your overall value as a human being judged by how many dollars you can trade for hours and what sacrifices are you willing to make to have stuff. I had never really had to pay a bill in my adult life. I always had someone else to take care of the details for me.

CHAPTER NINETEEN
STARTING OVER AS A MORTAL

By this time I had lots of good answers but I was broke, homeless and trying to decide what was next for me now that I wasn't an apostle and I had wasted fifteen years of my life in the church when I could have been getting help, counseling and treatment for mental illness instead of running around completely out of my mind fighting demons, talking to angels and promoting this kind of insanity to others. I felt so guilty and ashamed, I felt lied to and molested, I had been diagnosed years before and chose to believe Gods word instead of trained and educated healthcare professionals.

I was attending psychiatric outpatient care at my local MHMR, having both my children screened and counseled while trying to adjust to five kinds of new medications. I was by myself with no support because all my friends and wife refused to believe that I was mentally ill because of the effect that it would have towards their own beliefs. Every time I passed a church I was angry and every time I heard their unrealistic bible based bullshit I just wished they could accept my illness and start supporting me, but no Christian could ever accept a pastors willing decision to choose Hell and a life separated from God and heaven for a diagnoses of mental Illness.

When I left the church after fifteen years of faith and service to the cross, I was so mentally ill that I applied for some financial aid and after a psychiatric review and an explanation of my former Christian Beliefs, I was given full social security benefits for being completely mentally disabled and no longer able to work or function in society.

I returned to Jaco, Costa Rica where I live in a surfer hostel by the beach and protect myself and my son from the good intentions of others. I stay completely out of contact with the Christian world I once knew and segregate myself from the Christian Nation of my home land.

In Costa Rica the evangelical movement didn't really go over and the people did not let the Catholic church mandate the rules of society, so for the most part it is a secular society where Christianity is not shoved down your throat.

Now days I'm just a mentally ill person struggling to survive day to day without having to be institutionalized. I smoke pot to stabilize the affects of my illness (which I can not do in the US) and try to take my medications, but sometimes they are worse than the illness, I walk up and down on the beach each day and sometimes go to the mountains and just look at the jungle, I have no real future now so I just try to enjoy life and I don't do much thinking about God or any metaphysical theologies that can induce psychosis. Although I live in paradise I still fight severe depression, anxiety, fear and even thoughts of suicide, but I am no longer tormented by imaginary demons from hell and I'm not killing myself and wasting my life trying to get to heaven.

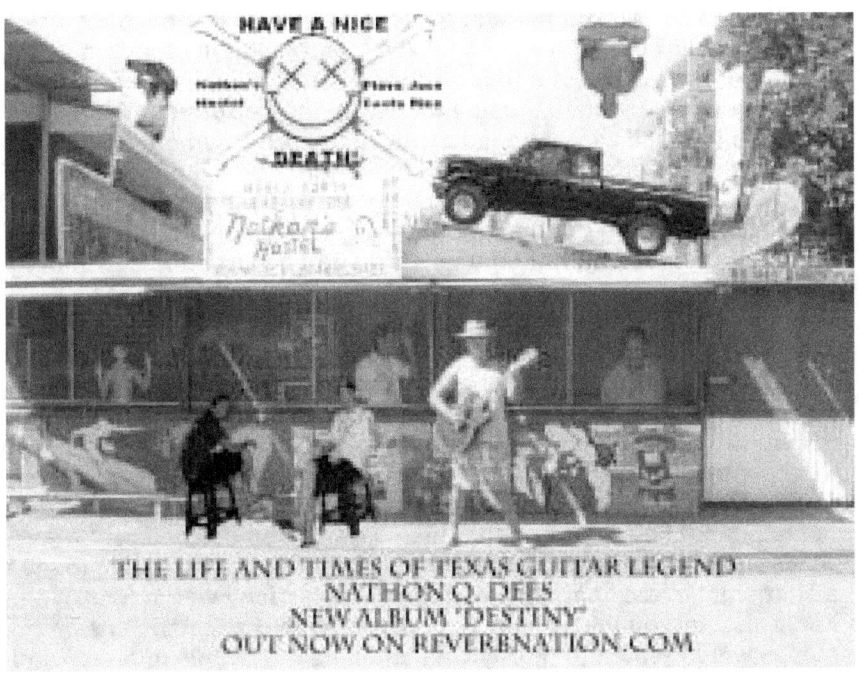

Nathon's Hostel Playa Jaco, Costa Rica

CHAPTER TWENTY
WHAT ABOUT THE MUSIC

Music was always a major player in this whole religious experience. Next to being with Athea or knowing God it was my greatest passion. I was very talented and music came to me easy. In schizophrenia as well as Bi Polar disorder the presence of brilliance comes in the form of mania and almost like an idiot savant music is second nature at times and it flows like pure logic and can totally consume you. It is a free flowing expression of inner feelings, thoughts and beliefs capable of identifying lifestyles, cultures, creeds and religions. Music was the most powerful force in the world and I was God's chosen oracle to speak through. When I played lead guitar in church it was if I would go into a state of trance and just start ripping improvisational leads over the Christian music that was being performed. When my solo was finished I would open my eyes to find the whole church Raising their hands to God and praising him. Some times when I played the whole crowed would start running around the church and freaking out, rolling on the floor, jumping up and down like punk rockers and speaking in tongues. This was an incredible performing experience to say the least. When I played my guitar God was speaking to his people through the music and I was his voice.
This was in fact the very reason that Satan Hated me and wanted me dead. You see as a teenager I had made a covenant with Satan to make me a Rock Star if I served him. Satan had used me for a puppet to distribute his lies and send people to hell and I was good at it. I was the Apostle Nathon Dees and I had been sent to earth as a messenger to be a light in a world of darkness and lead God's people out of the bondage that I had been ensnared in. Even when I played for Satan people still recognized my supernatural gifts and were drawn to me as a charismatic leader and wanted to be a part of my vision. Well with this war going on it was easy to understand that all musicians or muses were created to glorify God and lead his people in praise and worship.

Every musician that used his gifts for secular purposes was either willingly or unwillingly using his or her gifts for the promotion of Satan's Army and to keep people from the light of God.

Some musicians were willing and faithful servants of Satan and received great rewards here on earth for their service. Fame fortune and Glory even if it was only for a limited time. Other musicians chose to give their glory to God and humble themselves to a life of service to the music ministry and a reward in heaven. Leading God's people in super natural worship.

It was a sin to use your talents and gifts for the world. Music was supernatural and it was created to occupy your mind and heart with the praises of God in worship. Music was the most intimate form of worship and the ultimate expression of faith and love towards God. Every successful secular Rock artist had at some point made a choice to serve Satan. The greater their influence on the people the greater their reward would be here on earth. I was in competition with secular artist for the souls of the lost. I felt as if I owed it to God to use my music to spread the name of Jesus to the lost and I would pay God back one hundred fold to redeem myself from serving Satan. This battle for my soul and talents started at age thirteen and continued until I was thirty six.

I had been in a constant tug of war between God and Satan over my gifts and there was no middle ground I was either on one side or the other. Satan would play the secular music that I loved in my head while I was talking to God and I would have to pray in tongues and rebuke Satan in the name of Jesus until the music would go away and I could only Christian music in my head. Any time that I was not actively involved in something there was a running conversation in my head between God, Satan and the Holy Spirit. This conversation could take place twenty four hours a day forever if I let it. The voices would argue with each other about scriptures or events and failures in my life. I had to judge every thought that entered my head against my knowledge of the bible to see if the thought was from God or Satan. Satan had deceived the whole world into believing his lies and I was not going to let him take me down again.

This was completely acceptable behavior and is taught as Christian doctrine in your local church. This war inside my head and the constant struggle against the forces of darkness stood as the evidences of my calling and a sign of my spiritual gifts. I was completely delusional, out of my fucking mind and a very successful evangelical Christian minister with a powerful music ministry. The church loved me.

I possessed the ability to make things happen. We were at war and I was a soldier of God. Every decision that I made was in fact a life or death decision for some ones eternal soul. I possessed a divine gift of understanding and I got things done. That linked to good looks, talent, charisma and a beautiful wife and kids, hell who wouldn't want me on their team. I was supernatural officer material and I had worked my way up through the ranks rapidly. I was already making plans to start my own church and learning how to do it from men with million dollar ministries.

You might say "hey you're a smart guy, how could you really believe all of that stupid shit?". All I had to do to maintain this completely delusional train of thought was read the bible continuously and go down to my local Christian book store. Here at the Christian bookstore you can find thousands of books written by thieves, liars and mentally ill people. Schizophrenics and scam artist writing books on everything from speaking in tongues and demonic deliverance, to hearing and understanding God's voice.

You see I had done a tremendous amount of research and all of the extreme doctrines I believed in were from books that I had read written by very powerful and influential teachers in the Christian church. Names like Jerry Falwell, John Osteen, Walter Hallam, Kenneth Copeland, Kenneth Hagen, Oral Roberts, Jesse Duplantus, Joyce Myers, Creflo Dollar, Benny Henn and many more.

These were all very powerful and successful pastors with worldwide ministries that conclusively are either liars and thieves that are out to make money off of people or they are delusional mentally ill people that should be removed from their powerful and influential positions for the good of mankind.

CHAPTER TWENTYONE
STOP AND THINK ABOUT IT

A delusion is defined as a false personal belief based on incorrect inference about external reality and firmly sustained despite of what everyone else believes and despite what constitutes incontrovertible and obvious proof or evidence to the contrary (DSM -IV, p.765)
If you are hearing voices and seeing visions chances are you are suffering from some form of mental illness or you are on some good drugs. Not spiritual enlightenment and world domination but a nice padded cell and some lithium for starters to stabilize your mania. I had always been taught that science was the enemy of God and now I understand clearly that religion is the enemy of counseling and therapy as well as timely and proper diagnoses of the mentally ill. God does not audibly speak to people and there are no such things as angels or demons these are myths perpetuated by the lies of Christian Doctrine and exist only in the minds of believers. Separate yourselves from the delusional and insane and come out from among the deceitful and the deceived. Get the help you need and replace religious lies with medicine, counseling and facts.
The psychology behind Christianity is very extreme and the fact that so many people are so desperate for purpose and belonging or even social acceptance is absolutely amazing. It is a quite simple concept that if we are void of hope we find ourselves hopeless.
Hope in itself can be as simple as having a positive or hopeful attitude. In extreme or seemingly hopeless situations we can combine hope with faith which allows us to discount the natural and believe that the supernatural will take place.
Faith in God through Jesus gives us not only the hope that we might succeed in this life but offers us a second chance in the afterlife if we uphold the laws and practices that govern a religious based society or as it's referred to "The Kingdom of God on earth". You are born of flesh and are subject to the sin nature of flesh from birth and thereby condemned to hell, a hopeless situation, but through the death of the savior Jesus you can be redeemed from the curse of sin and saved from the torment of hell.

The grandiose delusion of heaven just isn't enough to persuade some people to join the church so the concept of hell was created and our adversary the devil was invented to manipulate people through fear into doing what was deemed as right and moral behavior. The problem with this Christian Nirvana/Damnation doctrine is that it establishes a course of action were there can be no truly self less act of Christian compassion because every action is motivated by reward or damnation. It is the equivalent of love enforced with a hand gun. It's kind of like marriage.

A covenant enforced by law and not love at least not unconditional love or God would make amnesty for all and not just those who accept his son. The problem is that amnesty for all would not leave a motivational factor for forcing people to do good and abstain from evil.

I can't even imagine what kind of constant stumbling block religion must create for mental health care professionals when they are trying to establish a working reality with a patient, if everything that the patient believes is a well documented lie with millions of followers to back it up. You have to give up heaven to get help.

When one becomes born again one creates an alternate reality in which you become a metaphysical spiritual being inside of a mortal body fighting against the mind will and emotions of man which are the enemy of God through the help of another metaphysical being the Holy Spirit. This is made possible because Jesus "God's Son" died on a cross and defeated Satan "the arch enemy of God" conquering sin in the flesh which allows you to become one with God through his Spirit.

These simple concepts alone are enough to signify insanity and one would need to be either completely ignorant or mentally ill to embrace such foolish and mid evil theories. Christian concepts like your mind and flesh being evil are no less than Spiritual Terrorism perpetuated by cruel and inhumane people.

Christianity condemns the entire world to death and subjects us to the daily crucifixion of our flesh to obtain self righteousness.

Christianity teaches us that the world only offers the lust of our eyes and flesh and the boastful pride of life and convinces us that we should trade our walk on part in the world and life for the afterlife in heaven and that our only purpose is to serve God.

CHAPTER TWENTY TWO
NEVER UNDERESTIMATE THE POWER
OF STUPID PEOPLE IN LARGE GROUPS.

Just being present in a atmosphere of people motivated by a common cause is a powerful force. From Amway to Hitler anyone who has ever experienced a large gathering orated by charismatic speakers has felt the power of acceptance or the experiential enlightenment of being a part of something more powerful than one's self. In a giant crowed full of people it is easy to be swept away in the emotional environment and make irrational decisions concerning faith and finance.
Eat shit, ten million flies can't be wrong.
If this whole Christian thing is about being loved, God sure asks for a lot in return. Love should be a balanced free flow of emotions flowing without inhibition or fear, towards someone or something, inspired by an inner emotional context of joy, elation or happiness and should be self motivated and a choice.
You should have the option of accepting or rejecting it but you can only be in it if you make a conscious choice to partake in it. The concept of being loved by God is an overwhelming idea to a hurting world of people wanting to be loved.
Well being loved by God shouldn't cost you your eternal soul if you did have one. God's love would be transcendent and present in all of creation flowing together in a universal oneness and harmony through the love of God for all. God's love shouldn't be a quest for world domination through evangelism using fear to manipulate people into a relationship. Nor would God's love require membership in a sectarian cult that's longing for the destruction of mankind so they can finally be segregated from the infidels and unbelievers and live in Nirvana for eternity with God while the unbelievers burn in hell with Satan. Let's not forget the other love of God where believers are sucked up into heaven and trained to kill and return to earth with Jesus to slaughter all the unbelievers left on earth.

Who needs that kind of love? That kind of thinking is insane.
Co dependant relationships with spiritual super beings that are hell bent on universal domination and the torture and destruction of all unbelievers in Hell in the name of love is pretty fucking weird if you think about it!!!

I'm only so mentally ill, I could only believe this horse shit for about fifteen years before I came to the realization that no rational individual with an education could ever accept these ancient myths as anything other than folklore and legend perpetuated by fear and ignorance.

To a Christian the concepts of an alternate reality are perfectly acceptable because they are already living in one. They feel shame because of the guilt imposed on them by a religious society and culture. There is a penalty for all those that fall short of the mandates of acceptable behavior and laws of their religion and therefore a need for redemption and forgiveness. Unfortunately to maintain this created reality of quasi holiness through redemption and forgiveness you must be brainwashed into believing the full content of Christian doctrine and belief including but not limited to the existence of :

SATAN: The former choir of leader of heaven who is now the King of Darkness after leading a rebellion against God and being cast down to be the evil ruler over the earth. He wears red pajamas and has a pitch fork.

Angels: Nine foot tall transparent warriors of light that work for God. Not pretty ladies or fat babies with wings

Demons: Fallen angels taking hideous forms that do the bidding of Satan their master and can inhabit humans and control their thoughts.

Witches: Humans that invoke the powers of Satan through the black arts or witchcraft. Both white and black magic.

Sorcerers: Much like the witches but more powerful and using the arts of sorcery for their magic.

Prophets: People chosen by God and given divine gifts of insight and prophesy and possess the ability to hear God's voice and cast out demons.

Curses: Evil words spoken over you that have power over your life.

Ancestral Curses: Curses imposed by God on entire families for generations.

Demonic Possession: Having your body play host to the spiritual embodiment of a demonic being that controls your thoughts or actions.

Faith healing: Believing that in the name of Jesus you can lay hands on the sick and they will recover.

Speaking in tongues: Possessing a spiritual language that Satan can't understand so that your spirit can send un hindered prayers to God and a supernatural gift that allows you to speak to people in languages that you don't know or understand.

Immaculate Conception: That Jesus is the only creature in the history of the planet, plant or animal that was ever conceived without a physical seed of it's own species being present and germinating.

Out of body experiences: Being removed from the physical body defying time, space, matter and gravity as you are either transported to another place, time or world or astral planning until you return to your body.

Resurrection: The re incarnation of inanimate dead human tissue into living breathing flesh. To bring the dead back to life.

Heaven: A spiritual Disneyland For Christians where you hang out forever and do nothing.

Hell: A land of molten lava and fire where you are tortured by Satan for not choosing to believe in Jesus no matter how good you were.

Now that you have accepted all of that all you need to do is understand the existence of a triune Godhead consisting of a father a son and a holy spirit which is the blueprint for the triune make up of man consisting of the body, spirit and soul which is the mind will and emotions of man.

If you can honestly say that you believe all that crap then you need to go to heaven and the church deserves ten percent of your income.

It seems as if it would be illegal to use Spiritual Terrorism to molest people's minds and suck them into a cult. Why aren't Christians subjected to the war on terror, they have the same twisted agenda as the people they are fighting. What is the difference, If I were blown up by a suicide bomber or if I were brainwashed and held hostage by a cult of radical religious extremist for fifteen years?

If I approached you on the street with a hand gun and threatened your life unless you accepted my belief or joined my quest for world domination than you might think you were in Nazi Germany and if you were a White nationalist during the time of Hitler you might even join enthusiastically.

Instead of a gun I'm going to approach with the number one selling book in history and claim that is Holy and inspired by God and that if you refuse to accept what this book has to say you will be condemned to hell for all of eternity and a social outcast here on earth living under the curse of sin. I would then began to explain to you how that you were a piece of shit unworthy of God's love because you were a sinner born of the flesh and that you were completely hopeless without God and I would explain that it didn't matter if you were a good person or not you were going down and that you would burn right next to murderers and pedophiles, rapist and criminals in hell for eternity if you chose not to believe what I believe.

That is Fucking Spiritual Terrorism and it is cruel and inhumane to sell these lies to mentally ill people looking for help. Trapping them with fear and then sucking out their money as they lure them towards heaven. We really can't afford to get rid of Christianity because it would soon be replaced by one of the other even worse religions and we would be pushed further back into the dark ages. It seems as if religion is a necessary evil almost like a divine military state forcing the masses into morality.

If Christianity were to be recognized for the Spiritual Terrorist group that they are, sucking people into their cult by brainwashing them through fear and manipulation, then as their leader Jesus was tried by a world tribunal for the atrocities committed by his cultic followers then I would in turn be tried as a war criminal just like the Nazis that believed in Hitler and were just following their orders. With the exception that history will reflect that Hitler was responsible for far less deaths than Jesus or Christianity in their two thousand years of murder and deception and it's not over yet. Idol worshiping spiritual cults in your home town. Churches performing rituals, baptisms, séances, laying on hands, faith healings, spiritual mapping, speaking in tongues and demonic deliverance and instead of a star of David, a swastika, pentagram or square and compass their symbol is a murder weapon, the cross of Jesus. Christian doctrine teaches that idolatry is witchcraft and an abomination to God, but the single most exploited cultic symbol of idolatry in the world is the murder weapon used by Christians as a pagan symbol of their faith. The presence of this cultic idol worshiping symbol is so prevalent in the US that I had to go to another country where I was not constantly subjected to the symbols of Spiritual Terrorism and to live without the constant reminder of the last fifteen years I had spent as a mentally ill hostage held prisoner by the lies of Christianity.

CHAPTER TWENTY THREE
WHAT'S LIFE LIKE NOW?

Here is where I am now. Back when I was in the states I was seeing a psychiatrist every two weeks, trying to come up with a cocktail of anti psych drugs that would stabilize my condition. I didn't attend any counseling for my condition because I understood perfectly what was happening and why. That made me a level three patient. Therapy and counseling were designed to help people understand and deal with what was happening to them. I had already discovered the answers on my own. Sitting around talking about things wasn't really going to help me much. I had been giving people counseling for years and I knew perfectly well what was up.

Reality Reconstruction Therapy.

What I needed to do was create an alternate reality where I could survive and take care of my children without being institutionalized. First I needed to remove the stressors that cause the anxiety, mania and psychosis. To do this I had to remove myself from the fast paced American culture and the Judeo/Christian society. No churches no Christians and far enough away from Athea that she would have to come find me this time and prove once and for all that she was totally committed to our love and to acknowledge the fact that we were both mentally ill. No more car or insurance or electric bills or pressure to be anything other than a mentally ill person. I moved back to Jaco, Costa Rica where I don't even know what day it is most of the time. I live in a tropical paradise where the mountains meet the ocean. If retiring in a tropical paradise is the greatest thing you can achieve in life then I'm not a failure after all because I'm here and you're not.

I had already lived in Costa Rica for nine months the year before and I knew that to live in Costa Rica legally all that I needed was a six hundred dollar a month US pension check to have pensionado residency. To get this pension I needed to apply for SSDI at the social security office. The qualifications for receiving the pension were that you must have paid into the social security program for at least five years within the last ten years, I had that.

You needed to prove that you had not been able to support yourself for over a year and have others that could sign an affidavit that they helped care for and support you during this period, I had that.

Most of all you needed to prove that you were permanently disabled and could no longer perform the task or trade that you had in the past and could not be retrained. Well by the time I got to this point I was so messed up on the meds they were giving me for the mental illness that I could hardly function at all. I had a diagnoses from the HMMR psychiatrist, from my local doctor and from the Veterans administrations psychiatrist and I knew a great deal about my condition so when the day came for my psychiatric review from the social security doctor I passed with flying colors and my statement didn't call for any review dates. I was permanently mentally disabled for life. They gave me eight hundred dollars a month for me and two hundred dollars a month each to my two children until they reached eighteen years old. Of course this was only enough money to live in absolute poverty in the US but in Costa Rica It was more than enough money to live comfortably and it was perfectly legal.

The day that I got my first pension check I went and got the words SCHIZOAFFECTIVE DISORDER 295.7 tattooed on my left fore arm inside of a yellow warning sign. This was my statement to the world "leave me alone, it's over, don't follow me I'm not the messiah I'm mentally ill. I finally once and for all knew who and what I was and had a government seal of approval. The tattoo also stands as a constant reminder not to try and be normal or have a life or a girlfriend or goals or ambitions because I'm fucked up and I can never win.

The most I can ever be is a mentally ill person that is subject to delusion. Jaco is a two mile stretch of beach surrounded by volcanic formed mountains that flow into a lava reef at each end. On one side jungles and mountains on the other side a popular surfing beach on the pacific shoreline.

Here in Jaco all I have to do is survive from day to day. It's not even like a real town in some ways, it's more like a carnival or amusement park for tourist, surfers and back packers. More and more wealthy outsiders keep showing up and exploiting this little town.

I think that in one or two more years Jaco will become the Las Vegas of Central America. There are eight new condominiums under construction at this time and real estate has become like gold. I will stay here as long as I can and then move on to the next surf village. During the high season there are thousands of visitors here from all over the world and I meet new people all the time. It's a party town with a festive flare. Gambling and prostitution are legal here and you can smoke all the pot that you want and no one cares. Almost all of us ex pats are alcoholics because it's easy to sit around and drink all day when you don't have to work anymore.

I live here with my dad and we run a surfers hostel on the beach. Having schizophrenia sometimes makes running a hostel the hardest thing I've ever done. Sometimes I get afraid of people and I don't want to meet any one new. Every time I meet someone they want to know my story, then they can't believe that I'm mentally ill or they feel awkward. If they are rock-n-rollers or stoners they usually understand and admire me for escaping the US and surviving my illness.

Like most Bi Polar musicians and artist I don't take my meds if there is any way I can avoid it. I hold off taking my anti psychotics until I hear voices telling me to kill myself. When the voices come I take lots off sleeping pills and I take Risperdone. When I wake up the next day there are no more voices. I am so used to having suicidal voices in my head that we make a running joke about me killing myself.

It's just like fighting demons but now I know that the demons are me. They are random messages of self destruction created by my mental illness. They can come on at any time and for any reason but all you have to do is not agree with them. You don't argue with the voices you just don't agree after all it's just bad brain signals. I don't date or go out and I don't sleep with the prostitutes even though they are really nice girls. Jaco is completely full of beautiful girls from all over the world. I enjoy the company of women and I would like to have a relationship but there is no way that I could ever be with some one that didn't know and understand my illness and willingly accept some of the extreme difficulties that my illness presents. There is only one girl I want to be with but she will have to be delivered from the lies of Christianity and leave the US to be with me. If this were to happen I might be encouraged to try again but short of being with Athea there is nothing in this world worth committing myself to and being sucked into an alternate reality or delusion when I know and understand that I am mentally ill. As long as I can survive in a reality where all I have to do is not kill myself, I win as long as I stay alive. If I forget that I am sick and I can't do the things I used to, then I am subject to mania and delusion. I know it will end in a crash and I will be more susceptible to suicide.

As long as I don't try then I can't fail and there is no reason to be depressed. There is no dishonor for me in this because no one could have tried harder to overcome a handicap than I have. If this handicap were physical, short of having my own pity party there would be nothing that could stop me from achieving my goals, But it's not; it is mental and I can not trust my own mind or emotions. To succeed you must believe and I realize that just because I see it or think it doesn't make it real and that there are a million alternate realities taking place with every thought in every mind in every second of every day. Any one of these realities can become truths to those who choose to believe in them and merely alternate perceptions of reality that I refuse to commit to, just thoughts or ideas no more.

I have a great deal of difficulty talking to my dad because at sixty nine years old he still has not come to grips with his or my schizophrenia and is constantly trying to suck me into his delusions. When I first wake up and say hello to him he instantly starts talking about money and business. We are both retired and we don't need to earn money but he just won't stop trying to make money. He spent what money we had left from the sale of our motel in Texas building me a business that I don't want and can't operate.

My dad just doesn't understand or believe that I'm mentally ill and that running a business is a total nightmare to me. I would much rather kill myself that be forced to live in a world of numbers always trying to destroy me. Taxes, payroll, inventory, rent, licenses, liabilities, advertising and bills, bills, bills.

He has been a very driven and successful person all his life and he just does not realize that I can't bring his visions to reality any more like I always had in the past. Before all he had to do was come up with an idea and fund it and I would do what it took to make it happen and we would share the profit.

Now even if I built a business I can't run it. When I deal with money figures I short out and that's all my dad lives for is to play the game of business. I didn't come back to Costa Rica to make a business this time I came here to hang out a while and try to enjoy life before I killed myself or completely lost what's left of my sanity. When I think about money I hate life and want to die.

Money has always been my enemy and no matter how much I made it was never enough. Now that I am mentally disabled and receive a pension I don't have to deal with the devaluation of my life through earnings as long as I live in a weaker economy than the US and can afford to live and care for myself.

Here in Costa Rica my rent and all of my bills combined are less than my electric bill was in Texas. I don't have much by standards in the States but to the Costa Ricans I am a Texas business man who is retired and still makes more than the average household earns. I am an artist and a musician and I am a master craftsman in many fields of construction but it is against the law for me to work, both as a term of my disability pension and my residency, so I don't.

I couldn't do it anyway, I just can't handle the stress any more. Just thinking about being involved in a large project causes me to become confused and scared. Not only of failure but that my next short circuit might be my last. After my last nervous/psychotic breakdown I realized that it was getting harder and harder to rebuild myself and that each time I returned the effects of the illness were worse. I have seen the leading edge of dementia and I understand how extreme the effects of schizophrenia can be. It has become my full time job to prevent myself from going there permanently or taking my own life just to end the struggle for sanity.

Caring for my dad and training my children Aaron and Natolie to cope with this disorder are my last obligations in life. I don't owe anyone anything. I have paid my debt to society, to God and to country. I was a faithful and loving husband but for now my wife has chosen Jesus over me. I was a patriot and a soldier but now the only cause worth fighting for is my own survival. I was a counselor, prophet and a priest for a God that didn't exist leading blind and foolish people astray in the name of hope. I never gave up trying until I realized that I had been disqualified from the game before I ever started. I never really had a chance to succeed or be normal, I had an abnormal brain in a world of normality.

CHAPTER TWENTY FOUR
LET'S TALK ABOUT MENTAL ILLNESS

The DSM-IV has become the bible for me now. It is as far as we know the truth. It is my salvation and the answer to life as I know it. If I study and indoctrinate myself in the scientific theories of neurological disorder then I truly arm myself against demonic attack and the forces of darkness. When knowledge and understanding are introduced superstition and ignorance fade into obscurity. When I was involved in Christianity I very seldom took the word of another pastor or teacher without researching the subject matter myself and developing my own theories before I reached a conclusion. Eating the watermelon and spitting out the seeds.

Un fortunately Christianity is based on circular reasoning so all of the opinions, commentary and alternate views were still all based on the same subject matter, the bible. As long as the bible is held as a standard of truth in your life and you hold the fundamental belief that it is inspired or holy, you commit yourself to a modified perception of reality where acceptance of delusional thinking is a requirement of faith. This certainly is not the prescription you would want to give someone that is subject to delusion.

If psychiatrist had the same motivation as pastors there would be a greater number of people that believed in mental health, but it's not a doctor's job to convince you of his diagnoses and his area of training is science and not salesmanship.

No one really wants to believe that they are mentally ill but everybody wants to believe that there is some other option, God.

When I cracked open my first book on Bi Polar disorder and started reading it I wept like the day that I found Jesus because I knew I had found the truth. It wasn't written in old English it hadn't been translated from ancient scrolls it wasn't holy or inspired by God. It was simply a book written by a doctor that explained to people what every MD practicing medicine in the field of mental health already knows. They might not know everything, but the data, symptoms and diagnostics available in that book were so self evident that after reading it I knew for an absolute fact that I was mentally ill and needed help and I wasn't going to get it from a church.

Hell I was the guy who counseled other people. As a clergy member I was a licensed counselor, I knew a great deal about human behavior. I was basically a mid evil psychologist practicing under a non sanctioned license. Most people don't know it, but pastors, priest and religious counselors are not required to hold any state license at all. They may have a license issued by a church or seminary but that license is only subject to the sect or denomination that they work for. In Texas there is no state licensing agency and there are no pre requisites what so ever. Even if they are degreed it is usually from a non affiliated Christian University that teaches religious doctrine instead of scientific theory. In fact I have often heard Pastor Walter Hallem publicly discourage the youth of his congregation from going to secular universities where they would be subject to the lies of this world. You know, lies like medicine and science.

You must always keep in mind that every licensed practitioner of medicine must be state board certified and have successfully completed a minimum of eight years of college plus internship. That's why religious counselors offer you free counseling and doctors charge you money. If a religious counselor can help you he gets 10% of your gross income instead of $100.00 per hour, not to mention brownie points in heaven.

Believing that I was not mentally ill in the name of Jesus wasn't going to make me well, but by believing that I was mentally ill sure answered a whole lot of questions that I had been trying to answer for decades. Why wasn't I normal and what the fuck was going on with my brain. It was almost embarrassing to think that everything that I had done for the past twenty years was because I was completely delusional. It was a leap of faith but I was completely sold on "juvenile onset, chronic, rapid cycling, Bi Polar 1 disorder", but I knew there was more.

I had been continually delusional and could easily experience mania and severe depression in a single day. I had been delusional for years at a time. The things that I read about normal Bi Polar symptoms made its victims look like sissies compared to the shit going on in my head but everything else was right on the money.

Let's keep in mind that I'm researching this in the wake of my last nervous or psychotic breakdown on my own, living in Art's Garage on a couch, isolated from all help because everyone I knew that could help me was a Christian. At this time I was pivoting on the edge of reality and then I got a book on schizophrenia.

After I read and understood the depths of psychosis and how severe the illness could become I was afraid. I understood that if I did not get a firm grip on reality that I was going to check out and not come back. I did not have the more severe symptoms of schizophrenia but I had a more consistent state of audio and visual hallucinations than present in Bi Polar disorder.

These symptoms were constant and accompanied mania, depression and good times too. Bi polar disorder normally cycles and these cycles can be monitored and mapped to some degree. My mania lasted until I crashed, I could live in a completely delusional based manic state of shamanistic euphoria for years at a time. When depression came and it did, I entered into a multi dimensional spiritual battle with Satan and his demonic forces until I defeated him through the power of Jesus.

I'm not shitting you at all, that's the way it was.

A lot of articles that I've read say that the term Schizoaffective Disorder is a catch all term that doctors use when they can't make an affirmative diagnoses. In my case I concluded the diagnoses myself before I ever saw a doctor. I knew that it was the only logical diagnoses for my condition. Well I wasn't a doctor, I was a researcher and a damn good one. I had just been researching the wrong curriculum for the answers. I had wasted fifteen years researching ancient fairy tales and religious commentary looking for the answers to everything.

When I took the next step and read a college level psychology book I understood everything. I didn't agree completely with everything but I damn sure knew a lot more than I did before. For instance; Freudian theorem and traditional psychiatry almost take as much faith as religion to believe, but the cognitive theory and neurosciences that have evolved from the early mental health sciences are no longer concepts and theories as much as they are accepted scientific fact. You see I'm not talking about sitting on a couch talking about your parents and trying to reach a hypothesis based on environment, experience, culture or upbringing. I'm talking about the fact that your brain has been genetically altered by some means and now your neurotransmitters are malfunctioning either too much or too little too fast or two slow. Dopamine, Serration, Glucosemines and their ability to flow through your synopsis.

It really is that simple and there's not a whole lot you can do about it. Every drug available for mental health disorders involving Bi polar and schizophrenia deal directly with these brain chemicals and their function. There's no great mystery here. The only question is how could this happen to me. Well although there are many camps on the subject of how, I think that other than coming to terms with yourself it is as irrelevant as wondering who made God or if chickens came before eggs. If you got it you need to deal with it and come to grips with reality. Let's take a look back any way just for shits and giggles.

1. I was born premature and had RH incompatibility syndrome. Research has shown links to the development of young adult schizophrenia in children born with this condition. Ok I'll buy that, I understand how that an undeveloped neuro-vascular system could affect the size of my synopsis and even the development of my responders.

2. Next I had a long history of crazy people on both sides of the family, My mom is depressive Bi Polar 2 and my dad is an absolutely amazing psychotic person, brilliantly twisted in a world according to himself but a great guy none the less. So I am a genetic candidate for both disorders if it's transferred through heredity.
OK I can buy that too, but wait there's more.

3. Remember the two brain concussions what about just plain old brain damage we can't rule out that.
So we've covered heredity, prenatal development and pre adolescent head trauma. If it were not for the fact that I personally know from my own understanding , experience and memory that I experienced hallucinations, out of body experiences and delusion as a small child I could not rule out the possibilities of drug induced psychosis.

4. Some researchers believe that Marijuana can induce schizophrenic affect and this is research and I can not rule out the possibility because I smoked Pot. You can go to .RxMarijuana.com and you will find a research study on the use of cannabis as a mood stabilizer in Bi Polar disorder. There is anecdotal evidence and a need for more clinical research.

My mom and dad didn't smoke and they were mentally ill and my sister didn't smoke and she was mentally ill. Everyone else that I knew that smoked it wasn't necessarily mentally ill so I wrote it off as more anti marijuana bullshit. The effects of mind altering drugs on normal people are much different than those of a person with an altered mind.
I have never experienced the affects of marijuana described in the DSM-IV or other medical journals. For me the effect of marijuana

stops the psychosis. The lulling or stoned affect experienced by a normal person is just enough to stop the voices so I only hear a single thought process. Kind of like a Spam blocker on the Internet. Pot has the ability to bring me out of a depressive suicidal episode in minutes instead of days. When normal people smoke pot they can become unmotivated. I suffer from delusions of grandeur and run the risk of psychosis and mania, marijuana stabilizes my thoughts and allows me to reason and prevents mania and anxiety. When I moved to Costa Rica I learned for the first time that Marijuana doesn't cause paranoia, getting busted in the States does.

In Texas if you or anyone in your household have ever been busted for pot, any amount, at any time in your life, you are completely ineligible for any state assistance including food stamps, prescriptions or psychiatric care from the HMMR, but you can get benefits if you are an illegal alien. Go figure that, sorry Charley no help for you Pot Heads !

Remember neuro science? While high doses of Delta 9THC of up to 50% found in today's hybrid hydroponics have been found to cause temporary psychotic affect in schizophrenia patients, regular sativa with lower levels of THC contain other canibinoids like CB1 and CB2 that manipulate canibanoid receptors in the cerebral cortex that effect Bi polar disorder by blocking serotonin receptors .

Wow, how about that.

So is marijuana the cause or the cure ?

I say marijuana keeps me from killing myself and is a whole lot better than the $ 1000 dollar a month prescription cocktail I was taking in the states that almost killed me. Zanex withdrawal was one of the worst experiences of psychosis in my life. Thanks Doc.

But I had much bigger fish to fry.

Numbers 5. 6. And 7.

From the time that I was thirteen until my Christian salvation at twenty I had done enough

5. LSD (acid),

6. MDMA (ecstasy) and

7. Psilocybin (mushrooms)

to have flown to the moon and back a couple of times, in fact I think I might have.

The point is that if all the other prevailing factors weren't in place I was still a candidate for HPPD or Hallucinogen Persisting Perception Disorder.

Guess what, this disorder has the same exact symptoms and treatment as, You guessed it; Schizoaffective disorder 295.7.

Do you get the point yet I had seven different valid possibilities of why I had the disorder and all I had to do was accept the fact that I had it, not figure out how.

I do know that if you have an HPPD diagnoses you don't get a government pension or disability benefits and if you have Bi Polar or Schizophrenia you do, so don't blame the acid if you want to get help. Besides the results and the treatments are the same regardless of what causes the illness the only difference might be in the therapy stage if you have issues to deal with in understanding and acceptance. It's a heavy trip to think that you're mentally scared for life because you partied to hard as a teenager but you can't rule out the possibility.

I personally believe that since the psychedelic drugs affect the 5 HT responders in the cerebral cortex that mimic the effects of these type of mental disorders it is obvious that when in later life someone experiences similar effects without the presence of the outside stimuli, they naturally assume that they are experiencing a relapse of their past drug induced experiences. For a person who has experienced the affect of mind altering drugs it would be easy to correlate the similarities between a psychedelic trip and the effects of psychosis. In fact how better could you explain a hallucination than to compare an acid trip.

Well I never had a bad trip and I never had a negative experience on mind altering drugs, but I had been running from ghost and demons since I was a child. It was depression and mania that led me to drugs in the first place.

I had a pre disposition for co morbidity long before I fucked up my brain on drugs and alcohol if the heredity guys were right and besides there is still a couple of million people who never did drugs and have schizophrenia and millions of people that have taken mind altering drugs that don't. Just like researching the bible you can't conclude a theory without substantial supportive evidence and unless every person that ever tripped on acid developed HPPD there is no conclusive evidence to show that this rare group of individuals who are diagnosed with HPPD were not already predisposed candidates for schizophrenia or Bi Polar in the first place and a doctor can not tell the difference. You just get labeled as a burn out and you don't get a pension check because you were misdiagnosed.

Ok so you're mentally ill what now?

Understanding and knowledge have been the only help that I have had since being diagnosed and leaving the United States. Educating myself about my illness along with marijuana treatment and living on the beach are what I have done to save myself from myself. I have never spent a day in counseling because, once you've read the counselors instruction manual it's kind of like exposing the Wizard of OZ and seeing behind the curtain. I had already dealt with all my psychological issues through Christianity. You know forgiving your father and loving yourself and all that bullshit. I taught that crap to other people for years, I was already completely past all that way before I had ever seen a psychiatrist. I am really thankful that Dr Kathy at my MHMR realized that and never patronized me. He respected the fact that I had diagnosed myself and done my research and immediately classified me as a level three patient and didn't recommend therapy. I mean sure it's great to get things off your chest but at $100 bucks an hour you can go smoke a joint and write it down in a journal or write a book, it's good therapy.

Instead of just listening unfortunately most counselors and therapist want to help you, so after you finish whining they give you advice. Lots of it is good advice, but any one that is from a Judeo/Christian background whether a licensed practitioner or a clergy member is going to give you advice and recommendations based on religious theology that will only perpetuate your delusions and keep you in a state of psychosis.

Therapist that encourage their patients to get involved in faith or religion are simply passing off their patients to a world of delusion where they can function in a robot society of fairy tales instead of healing them with truth and reality. Not to mention the tremendous liability involved in prescribing a treatment of un safe and unhealthy religious involvement that promote trains of thought that induce prejudice, fear, psychotic behavior and much worse.

Remember hypnotism is not a cure for mental illness and hypnotizing yourself to believe that Jesus healed you is not going to do anything for your but extend your period of psychosis and make it more difficult for you to keep a firm grip on reality. If you feel like you need to be forgiven, for God's sake forgive yourself, after all sin is established by religion in the first place and creates a ubiquitous cycle of acceptance and denial.

You haven't fallen short of anything except a lot of stupid prerequisites established by a religious society and the expectations of others that do not understand that you are mentally ill and therefore separate and different than the cultural norms of society. Now that's not a license to shit on everyone but you must understand that you will never be like all the other kids. You're different and unique. You are one percent of the world's population and can not ever be expected to fit into the norms of any society without being subject to delusion. The societal standards set forth as normality for everyone else, is a living hell for me and an unrealistic goal that I can never achieve. It's not my fault it's just the way it is.

I am mentally ill. On the other side of the coin you are herded along into the other category where you are segregated from society with the severely handicapped, the mentally retarded and the insane because you have a mental disability. Mania and delusion can be contagious when you get around other mentally ill people and a mental institution is not the healthiest place in the world to be. Helping other people can be very therapeutic and rewarding for some but for now I can only help myself and my children. I hated sitting around the MHMR waiting to be seen with all the other crazy people. I wanted to talk to my doctor, get my meds, talk to the kid's doctors and counsel with them and then get the hell out of there.

CHAPTER TWENTY FIVE
CHARASMANIA
PHYCHOSIS AND RELIGION

I realize the need for a more comprehensive study of some of the theories and experiences discussed in the book. This was as I intended it to be, my story and nothing else. I felt no need to go into great detail about the doctrines and scriptures referenced in the book because I didn't want to lose the interest of the non doctrine savvy readers and still get my point across. I realize to many of you both agnostic and Religious alike you are searching for absolute truths and definitive answers and need to know everything there is to know about something and I admire that.

The Bible teaches us to study that we may show ourselves approved, a workman that doesn't need to be ashamed and it's right in that respect. We only need to stand in shame when we let ourselves remain in the vast expanse of ignorance necessary to sustain an unrealistic delusional existence perpetuated by the ancient ramblings of madmen written down two thousand years ago.

I will not attempt to prove whether Jesus was God's son, or resurrected or validate the stories of the bible because honestly those points are aimless and non productive. I have spent years arguing Christian apologetics and defending the Christian faith and what I'm attempting to reveal is far beyond the envelope of arguing doctrine with religious fanatics.

For example; We all go see " Star Wars" together, afterwards we all go to the coffee shop and you guys are discussing maters within the context of the film (The Bible GET IT!) and we are discussing George Lucas (Realizing of course that it was only a story, written by a man). I think it's a good example and an explanation of why this book is far beyond proving or disproving the Bible, but will attempt to show clearly that if you believe the Bible with all of your heart and practice it's doctrines and apply it's theories to your life you will ultimately commit yourself to a life of psychosis and delusion.

The other day I was pondering a phrase as I so often do as I remembered the words of Mr. Fred Rogers from Mr. Rogers Neighborhood on PBS (a Presbyterian minister I might add).

Mr. Rogers always said "Welcome to the world of make believe" when his show came on. The World of make believe or to make the world believers, to make believers of the world or as Mark 16 said "Go Ye into all the world making believers". I know that this is just a funny play on words but the point is, unless you are indoctrinated as a child or someone takes advantage of you during a period of duress it takes a professional evangelist (a trained sales person) and the peer pressure of other believers such as friends and family to make you accept the Bible as anything more than just a compilation of old stories and fables. In fact; I can think of no other book that anyone could ever hand you that would hold the weight of eternal damnation or nirvana upon your acceptance of it's content. Well not necessarily, I was handed a psychology book and told that if I didn't accept what it had to say I would in fact be committed to a life of Hell and agony on earth, as long as I continued to believe the Bible and fuel my delusions with the spiritual subject matter held within the context of Bible Based Christian doctrine.

You see I came to a point in my life where I had to stand in a place beyond the realm of merely believing. I was forced to make a choice between choosing to believe the Bible or my interpretation thereof and living in an unreal parallel dimension where I spoke to God ,Angels and Demons and was tormented by Satan or accept the fact that none of these things were real and what I was experiencing was in fact psychosis fueled by my beliefs in Christianity and perpetuated by religious practice. Now I'm not saying that Christianity is the cause for my schizophrenia or anyone else's, What I am saying is that the modern day church is nothing more than a free outpatient clinic for the mentally ill (free except for 10% of your income) and that professing to believe in the bible actually qualifies you to be mentally ill by today's modern diagnostic standards.

Although in the past unfortunately, choosing to believe in the bible meant social acceptance, eternal fire insurance and a ticket to heaven as well as the very popular belief that you would be tried and killed for witchcraft because you were an unbeliever and not a member of the local church. That was always a popular motivating force.

In today's more modern world people are finally more inclined to choose to be labeled sane as there is a much greater stigma about being mentally ill than there is about going to hell. I had to choose the former of the two. I could no longer exist in a world where the Bible was true and protect my state of mental well being.

Either the Bible was a lie and there aren't parallel dimensions of metaphysical beings warring for our souls or I was condemned to a life of torment and anguish fighting a never ending battle with Satan and his forces defending righteousness and the cross of Jesus for an ultimate reward in the afterlife. The answer was clear to me, I had already spent fifteen years fighting demons and listening to God's voice and when I made a decision to step out in true faith and denounce Christianity just to see for myself what the truth really was. This is not to be taken lightly. To take such a stand in the search for ultimate truth in itself is a messianic quality. I basically committed spiritual suicide forfeiting the grandeur of heaven and even eventually destroying my marriage and career to see once and for all what the definitive truth of this matter was.

In my case I found out that I was mentally ill and needed help. In your case hopefully you will just discover that you're wasting your life and spending all of your time and money throwing it all away on ancient myths, legends and folklore. If Christianity was a club and we all just tried to do good things like Jesus, it would be cool but it's not. Christianity by definition is a sectarian religious cult movement just like all the other religions and as a term of faith you are requested to believe that the Bible is in fact the inspired word of God which in turn leads to a profession of belief in absolutely impossible concepts of metaphysics that unknowingly traps us in a world of unrealism and delusion.

The study of secular theology and psychiatry where taboo in the church. Just as early Catholicism taught that the holy scripture could only be interpreted by the priest who led to the Protestant reformation, modern day theorist can only substantiate their claims of absolute truth by forbidding the study of secular reasoning, science and psychology. When knowledge and education are applied to myths and fables, truths are analyzed under a different spectrum of light casting shadows on archaic theories once taught as absolute truths.

It was only when I removed myself from a Judeo Christian society and culture that I realized that what I held as absolute truths were merely the embodiment of my own personal beliefs and a reflection of the programming that I had received from a group of irrational individuals that's sole purpose for existence is for all the world to join them in their quest for universal dominion and oneness with spirituality (taking over the world in Jesus Name). "That every knee shall bow and

every tongue shall confess on both heaven and earth that Jesus Christ is Lord to the glory of the father".
In the words of the modern day philosophers Cheech and Chong "Wow that's some heavy shit man!".
To push the rational brain beyond reason is the essence of spiritual belief, but to engage in un healthy psychotic behavior that stands outside of rational thought such as forcing oneself to believe concepts far beyond ones personal scope of reference and filling in the blanks with faith does not constitute a true personal belief but more of the existential leap of faith. If you were to say, wait and let me go to college and study history and psychology before I conform myself to such an unrealistic belief system, you would need to be discouraged from illuminating yourself in the ways of the world and the lies of Satan, because those books are secular and products of the mind of man which is the tool of Satan at enmity with God. No one would ever invite you to openly discuss the possibility that anything in the Bible was not true because it would destroy the very foundations of Christian faith.

CHAPTER TWENTYSIX
BEFORE WE REALY SAY GOODBYE

Before we say goodbye I would briefly like to touch on a few personal points that were discussed in the previous chapters. Although I come off as being pissed off some time (and rightly so) I'm not . I'm not a Christian Basher, in fact I will be the first to tell you that some of the finest people that I have ever met have been Believers. I spent fifteen years of my life ministering to the needs of others and leading untold thousands to the knowledge of Christ through personal witness, preaching, street ministry and music ministry and yes Demonic Deliverance Ministry too.

Before I indoctrinated myself in basic Christian dogma, I had no moral guidelines or standards in my life and without the application of religious legalism enforced by eternal damnation I did not possess the personal will power necessary to keep myself from sin. But you know what, the Army was capable of achieving the same thing in just eight weeks of training but unfortunately both organizations request the sacrifice of your life as payment for this fine training. The gentlemen that wrote the books that I had read on Psychology paid for four years of university training in general applications before paying for post graduate and doctrinal studies equaling about ten years of college plus internship before they started spouting out their bias opinionated theories. So we can gather that the lessons of self preservation must come at a really high price.

Who of the three afore mentioned would have the purest motive ?

The motive of the Christian can never be truly pure. Christianity needs You to validate it's self because the greatest ruling factor in its favor is popular consensus. The beliefs of the Christian can only be validated on earth if you choose to believe them too. Their very plight against the odds of reality hinges on your acceptance of their belief, as a matter of fact it is so important that you will be condemned to Hell for not agreeing with them.

That's pretty serious! And just like it's the mandate of Islamic extremist to kill for jihad it is the Christian's mandate to convert or condemn all of mankind and this is his purpose for existence.

Next the Drill Sergeant. His motive is pure but certainly not in your favor. Oh he's your buddy and he'll take care of you but always remember that his primary objective is to develop a winning team of highly motivated killers. He can offer you a world of certain unarguable realism like his boot in your ass or you will die if you don't follow orders. OK here we go with absolutism again. Wasn't it the great philosophers DEVO that taught us that freedom from choice is what we really want?

As long as I am free from personal choice or decision I seem to excel. I wonder why that is? " NOT".

How many of you ever excelled in sports after your coach stopped yelling at you?

OK now the Psychoanalyst. If this guy misdiagnoses you it could destroy his career and potentially lead to a patients attempted suicide or death. Although he charges you a lot of money " Almost as much as a prostitute" he is forced to charge a lot to cover the cost of the mal practice insurance necessary to protect him against you when he tells you that you need help and you tell him that he's crazy.

Not only did I not have the motivation to put myself through ten tears of higher education, if I did, it sure as hell wouldn't be so I could sit around and talk to crazy people. Oh these guys are out to get your money " get for real " I only listened to other people's problems because the voices in my head told me to, I would have never done it for any amount of money. I hated being forced to have compassion on people that I thought were dumb asses. Remember I'm BI Polar. Explaining obvious problems to people with their head up their ass is not at all fun. Not to mention the real therapy that goes on with truly mentally ill people that are given a much better quality of life when under the care of a loving professional.

Now I'm out here on my own for the first time in 39 years. No wife, no Jesus, no God, no Drill Sergeant and not even a psychiatrist. They have all done their part and I have graduated everyone's course with flying colors. My wall is covered with pretty pieces of paper that say what a smart and great guy I am and list my many accomplishments. But just as eternal reward comes after this life is over. My illumination and understanding of life as I know it only came to me after the realization that I was Permanently mentally impaired and my perceptions of reality were distorted and not to be trusted. It also cost me the highest price to realize and believe this. Not only did I divorce my Christian wife who I love dearly, I had to leave the church, default heaven and be labeled as permanently mentally disabled to be in this popular club of unbelievers with no hope. But yet there is still hope for us.

Well in closing I would like to say good luck, if reading my story has benefited anyone in any way it almost makes it all worthwhile. Please don't take my word for the information that I've presented, research for yourselves and make your own determinations. Both the internet and the local library have a wealth of information available that can help you make the transition from an ignorant victim wandering in the dark to a proactive participant in your own recovery.

If you are a mental health professional, thanks. I hope that reading my experiences might offer you an alternate viewpoint or give you a different perspective in helping treat your patients. I know it has sure helped me.

If I could believe in anything I would choose to believe that my wife Athea might someday read this story and put down her cross, sacrifice the false reality of heaven and hell, denounce Christianity and come live with me in paradise. This like any other delusion is, and can only exist as a dream until reality is applied and action has occurred. Like so many others Athea's been brain washed for so long that Christianity has become her identity and she can no longer think for herself she can only quote bible scriptures and respond to the voices in her head that she believes are spirits.

Thank You.

The Rev Nathon Q. Dees
AKA Jaco Nate, Guru AkhNathon
Or Texas Guitar Legend Nathon Dees
NathonsPlace@aol.com

Rev. Nathon Dees ∾ Delusions of a ...: Rock n Roll Messiah

The Further Adventures of Texas Guitar Legend Nathon Dees

Delusions of a Rock N Roll Messiah

The Further Adventures of Texas Guitar Legend
Nathon Dees

This is the Second Book in The Texas Guitar Legend Series. In Delusions of a Rock n Roll Messiah you will join in the Adventure as the Rev. Nathon Dees leaves Jaco, Costa Rica to returns to the United States of Confusion, Recovers from Mental Illness and Ascends only to uncover the Greatest Conspiracy ever told with him Right in the middle of it. From playing Live Rock n Roll Guitar at Bike rallies to being thrown into a Government Maximum Security Psycho Ward and being stripped of all rights for no crime and no reason only to escape the Marshall Law New World Order that was taking place in the U.S. and return to Exile in Central America.

Chapter One
Goodbye Pura Vida

After spending four years living on the beach in a small coastal Village in Costa Rica, I had decided that it was a time for a change. I was till severely mentally ill but I had learned to overcome some of the more severe symptoms of my schizoaffective disorder. My daughter Natolie was already back in the States living with a friend Michael Klumpp and my son Aaron was fixing to be eighteen and wanted to move back to the United States so that he could finish school and get a driver's license.

About this time I heard from my old buddy Art Napoli who was now living in Arizona of all places. He simply asked me if I still wanted to play guitar and I said that I would love to be in a band again or to come play guitar with him. I made arrangements for my dad to take over my business in Costa Rica then Aaron, Don Cool and I left our super cool surfer village where we were safe from society and returned to the United States of Confusion.

You have got to understand why I left the states in the first place. Everything that I had been taught to believe in was a Lie and everyone that I knew back in the states was part of the conspiracy. Mania and depression themselves are very difficult to cope with, even in a controlled environment, like back in the US, how would I ever be able to adjust to the oppression and opposition that I would be met with back in the States.

When I arrived at the International Airport Houston Airport (IAH), on my lay over to Arizona, my ex wife Athea was there. She ran to me and held me like there was no tomorrow. We wept as we held each other tight then she asked me if there was any way that I could change my plans to come stay with her so that we could be together once more. I painfully told her no. For one, she had never supported me in my struggle with mental illness and still thought I was demon possessed and not mentally ill. More importantly, she was not the one that invited me to come back to the States or offered me a job, Art did. I caught my connecting flight and was on my way to Arizona to begin a new adventure and see what was next in life.

Art had always been a real player and this time he had once again out done himself. The gig in Arizona was a good deal so I started work the day after I got there making $30 per hour cash. I went from living on my small government check and having no money for years to making several thousand dollars a week instantly. I was adjusting to things the best way that I could but the reality of the matter was I was completely freaked out. Art had to basically take care of me in the since that I did not really even want to talk to other people and as long as Art took me to work, fed me lunch and told me the job detail I needed to work I was fine and could function. Here is the catch Art is bipolar too and he lives in a world of mania. He is always swinging a deal or making something happen. Well it turns out that the reason that we were in Arizona was because Art's old girlfriend Tammy had been transferred there. Well, that was OK, Tammy was super cool and she was my friend as well but that just wasn't enough for Art so he moved his other girlfriend, Sheila, in to Arizona to hang out with us too. Now, how long do you think it took for the two girls to figure out that he was seeing them both again in another state? Not long enough.

When the, double life double girlfriend, fiasco exploded on Art and the high paying construction job came to an end it was time to go back to Texas with our winnings and start our new Rock Band Called Ten Foot Hammer.

Chapter Two
Hello Texas

Aaron and I showed up in Austin Texas with an old 93 Ford F-150 that we had bought in Arizona from Art and enough cash to last a month or so. Well, since I had been a successful business owner, built and owned my own homes and was self employed I had no rental history, no employment records, no source of income, and no references. I had just spent the last three and a half years living on a beach in a third world country battling schizophrenia and I could not find a place to stay in Austin. Aaron and I went back to our almost home town of Dripping Springs Texas. The government had built some low income Apartments called the Springs but since there really aren't that many low income families in Dripping Springs because they can't afford to live there, the apartments were really kind of nice, especially compared to what we had been used to in Costa Rica. The lady at the "Springs" told us that she would give us a lease if my mom would cosign for us since we were home folk. Well this was the best news that we had got since we returned to the states. Aaron got a job at the school and I was traveling to Austin everyday doing odds and ends stuff for money and playing with a couple of bands trying to get something going. Meanwhile, Art was auditioning every drummer in town and trying to get something going with whoever he could when he introduced me to Guy Elder. Guy was cool enough but he was kind of a poser. I mean he was real enough and he was a bad ass drummer and road a Harley and was otherwise a really cool dude but he was a little drama queen and thought a little more highly of himself than he should when he wasn't beating himself up. Another fucked up Bi Polar Quasi religious Christian freak. Well, in order to get Guy to play drums for Art's " Ten Foot Hammer" band I agreed to play bass and Sing for Guy's band "Triple Tree", a 70's & 80's, classic rock cover band. Art wanted to play dropped D southern party music and hit the Local Austin scene but Guy was fed up with gigging bars and wanted to focus on motorcycle rallies and parties. Hell, I didn't care, I just wanted to jam. Well, after several months of preparation for both bands everything fell through on me. Our friend Ahmed Garcia was going to play lead for Triple Tree but Ahmed had already been working on his own solo hippie music and for years and was trying to manipulate Guy into playing for him. Well, Guy was secretly trying to manipulate Ahmed to play for his band instead and well Art he was trying to manipulate Guy through me to do his will so that he could have more than one drummer available that knew the material. So everyone fucked everyone else over because of their own selfish ambition and pride and everything blew up in my face. At the time I didn't really know how chicken shit Guy was so when he offered to take Aaron and I with him to College Station to continue with Triple Tree I jumped on it. I am thankful for what I achieved working with Guy and I had some good times in College Station but in retrospect I will have to admit that Guy his Buddy Chris and most of the people that I met in College Station are the biggest bunch of back stabbing liars that I have ever met in my entire life. It took three years of living with Guy and Jamming with him and Chris to realize the depth of their deception and lies. Nearly everything that they had told me was a lie. They knew every one in every band and were friends with Pantera and had toured the world. Ninety percent of it was all bullshit. It turns out that they were make up wearing fagot posers from the 90's that had only played locally and experienced very limited success. Hell they could not even book a gig, never showed up for practice, could not remember their parts, and did not do anything but criticize each other. They both sucked. Hell I grew as a musician because of them. Their lack of professionalism forced me to step up to the plate. I was originally just going to play bass and now I was doing the sound, lights set up and take down, playing lead and rhythm while doing the lead vocals. Chris was so dumb that he could not even remember which parts that he sang from gig to gig so I always had to sing his parts too. I was doing AC/DC, Judas Priest, ZZ Top, you name it we played it. It was all top 40 classic Rock and I played it with integrity.

When the gig went well it was all Aaron and I. I was the front man and it was my show.
Guy and Chris were really holding me back and it was time for me to go in a different direction.
(Art showed back up in the Picture and was willing to do the Ten foot Hammer gig again so we picked up and went back to Austin to hit the bar scene and play every week end.)

The House where we were living in College Station was a huge old mansion that we had rented from some friends of Guy's after we remodeled it. When we decided to move to Austin the same people had a house there so we remodeled it for them and moved in it. I had been seeing my psychologist the whole time that I had been back in the States. I was seeing Dr. Joan Clayton the head Psychologist at the VA Hospital and we had a very good working relationship. I was taking meds and sleeping most of the time and doing everything that I could to remain balanced. I also had enrolled in a program at Texas A&M University and was seeing a psychology student there named Anna. I had enrolled in a program called DARS (Department of rehabilitative services or something like that) and they were paying for me to go to college.

So let's get the gist of this. I was still pretty messed up. Still somewhat delusional and schizoaffective while rebounding back and forth from meds to no meds. I was going to college and taking psychology classes and playing in the band at night. The rest of the time I was either asleep or a brain dead zombie on the meds. We never had any money and we all really didn't get along very well. Art worked hard all day and when he came home before a gig the first thing that did was start a fight with Guy by telling him what a worthless piece of shit that he was. This always set the mood. Now Guy is all pissed off at Art and I have to load up all of the shit because they won't speak. This was and still is Arts modes' apparati.

He blames it on me and we both blame it on the Army and my dad Byron for making us into such assholes but when dealing with stupid people you almost have to subjugate them and beat them down or you can't use them. If someone is not your equal and you are in authority over them the only way to make them respect you is to make them fear you or dread you. I understand the concept completely but at this point in my life I am still looking for equals and not followers as it were. I don't want the stress and the power struggles and I out rank most people in intellect and ability any way so the last thing that you want to do with me is pull rank and start barking orders. At this point in life one of two things are going to happen I will smile at you and turn and walk away never to return or we will have a violent altercation. I tend to walk away quite often now days.

Chapter Three
College Station Crazy Train

The house in College Station was nearly 3000 square foot but it was old so no one wanted it. The fireplace was nearly six feet long and the house had huge rooms. Guy had his room down stairs that he only came out of for work or to jam. He was a recluse and always kept to himself. Art and Shelia were staying in the living room in front of the fire place during the winter and Natolie and Aaron had their own rooms upstairs. I also let Natolie's friend from school live with us so I could help her get through school. The music studio was the largest room in the house so I chose the smallest room. There was an office off to the side of the kitchen just big enough for a bed. This was my home. Ever since I lost my Quarter of a million dollar house in Wimberley, Texas that I had built for Athea, I had become a minimalist. So, if I don't have anything of value then you don't have anything worth taking from me. In Costa Rica I let Aaron and Natolie sleep in the house with air conditioning and I slept on the porch on a cot under a mosquito net. When I moved into the hostel I again took basically a closet and made a room out of it, more like a prison cell than a room. In my room I had a bed, a guitar and a surf board, this is where I found comfort. I would have coffee in the morning and take Natolie to school in an old Volvo that someone had given me. When Natolie was going to graduate even though I was poor I pulled all of my resources and did a big remodeling job in Austin then I bought her a Mercedes Benz 350SL Grey car and restored it. The car was a beautiful and worth a lot of money so I felt like I had finally dealt justice to Natolie. I had helped her get through high school and bought her a nice expensive car even though I was a mentally handicapped musician that she did not approve of. It only took two weeks for Natolie to totally destroy the car in a collision. She took an unprotected left hand turn at a four way intersection and was wiped out by another car. She wasn't injured severely but it still cost me nearly ten thousand dollars and a car that I had just rebuilt. My mom helped me to get Natolie another car and she soon moved out and went out on her own.

I had been talking to my ex wife Athea from time to time and we were getting along OK but she still refused to accept any responsibility for our divorce, she was still unwilling to accept my illness and insisted that the problems were spiritual in nature. I had known and loved Athea since I was thirteen years old and I just never really understood what a liar that she really was. She was in church every time that the doors were open and spent every day reading the bible and quoting scriptures. Yet, even though I was not good enough for her to love, she had sex with me every time I saw her. I never advanced on her sexually, every time we where alone she would have her way with me. Hell, nothing had changed, that is why I married her, that's what she was behind my back while we were together and that's what she was doing now. In fact she even had another boy friend that she lied to me about while she was seeing me and was pregnant with his Child..

Everything in her life was a lie and it took me nearly thirty years to understand how deep the rabbit hole went. The amount of time, love and devotion I had thrown away on this individual in the name of love. What a fool I was for believing in love one more time.

SATURDAY June 28th
Cindy's Hawg Hangout PRESENTS
LIVE ROCK n ROLL
FROM

TRIPLE TREE

70s and 80s CLASSIC ROCK

Chapter Four
Reprogramming my Cognition

Wrecked cars, broken relationships, deception and lies, everyone that I was involved with had major character flaws, lacked morality and acted as if they were normal. Hell, I was the one that was mentally ill I was the one seeing a doctor and going to counseling.

 Everyone claimed to be a Christian and go to church "except for Art" and they were all liars that had no foundation of truth in their lives. Guy would lie to everyone that he talked to on the phone and make up excuses for every short Cumming in his life. Chris was a lying instigating bastard that wouldn't know the truth if it hit him.
 Athea bless her heart was the biggest nut case liar that I had ever met and I had been in love with her since I was thirteen years old. Art was just a Bi polar psychopath on drugs, at least he had an excuse!

OK, so, I am the damaged one. I have schizophrenia, am I broken and can't be a part of society or have a job or a future? I am the only one with any moral character at all. I had walked away from religion time and time again in search of ultimate truths. I had shunned and refuted anything in my life that seemed to lead me in the wrong direction. I took great strides to avoid drugs and alcohol even though I was very susceptible to them. Sure, I was mentally ill but I was not morally ill. I still knew the difference between right and wrong.

Natolie directed me to a book Called "Cognitive Behavioral Therapy for Dummies" I read it and reprogrammed my mind in one week.

I felt that Natolie and Aaron secretly despised me and blamed me for all or the shortcomings in their lives. Guy was a complete liar and a back biting gossip queen, Chris was a liar and a Dirtbag " Guy Loved him and Chris could do no wrong in Guy's eyes". Everyone that said that they were my friend in College Station turned on me, robbed me and slandered me because of the lies that Guy and Chris had told them and I was eventually railed out of town.

When I finally left College Station there were eight false police reports with my name on them and I had done nothing to anyone and they were all lies.

You see after Ten Foot Hammer broke up I went back to Costa Rica to visit my dad.
Before I left my son Aaron had spoke to me and said " Hey pop I know that you have some problems and so do I but you still know how to do things because your dad taught you, I am twenty one years old now and I can't get a job making tacos." I had been feeding, clothing, and providing shelter for Aaron but since I was not in business anymore and not running jobs like I had my whole life I had never apprenticed Aaron on the Job like my father had so at twenty one he basically had no trade skills what so ever so when I returned home from Costa Rica I went to work to try and build a future for Aaron. After all, my son Aaron is the only one that had not lied to me or betrayed me since I had returned to the United States.

When I returned home from my visit with my dad in Costa Rica I left Austin and moved to Bryan Texas which was next to College Station and moved into another house that I had previously remodeled.
I went to work immediately. The day after I returned I was on a job. I rebuilt a porch and re roofed a house and then the next week Aaron and I built a car port while Guy was lining out a room addition on a restaurant. The whole time that I had been working with Guy for the last three years I let him think that he knew something and I tried to support him and make him feel better about himself, well that time was over and I was going to be Nathon again. When I took over the job and started doing all the work and dealing with the customer first hand Guy freaked out. He really did not know or understand who or what that I really was. He thought that I was a mentally ill handy man and did not realize that I was a professional craftsman and a home builder so when I stepped up to the plate it was embarrassing for him because he could not be the big man any more. I ran circles around him on the job and everything that I did was correct and finished and nearly everything that he did was flawed. Like I said before Guy was a poser so everything that he ever accomplished was on the heels of someone else. Well this time his dumb ass was exposed and everyone could see his folly in the open. I realized that because of my decision to try again and be somebody so that I could help Aaron, it

was going to destroy my relationship with Guy and that I really would be on my own for the first time in years. I had to come up with a plan and find a way to start and run a business that could sustain Aaron and provide him an income.

Chapter Five
I awoke the Genius Again

At this time I had been rebuilding an old guitar that someone had given me and I was building a face plate for it out of wood. When I finished the face plate I realized that there would be a market for such a product but I knew that in order to mass produce such an item I would need a CNC machine. I went to the internet and much to my dismay the CNC machines that I would need to start my business started at about five thousand dollars and I did not have that kind of capitol. I only had a couple of thousand dollars to live on off of the Restaurant job and I did not have Guy to help me anymore. That is when I saw a web site on building your own CNC machine and I started studying and researching the machines. Within a week I had completely invented designed and fabricated my own CNC machine and the computer hardware necessary to run it. I taught myself auto cad and tool path programming over the internet and I was up and running. My machine worked great and I was on my way to being a successful business man again for the first time since I had been diagnose with mental illness. When I built the CNC machine I rebuilt myself. I chartered a nonprofit business and got all of my tax ID's and permits and leased a booth at the local flea market where I would start selling my goods and taking orders for custom name plates and artwork that Aaron and I were making on the CNC machine. We were on our own and making money.

I came up with a plan to buy an old church in town and turn it into a trade school where I could get government grants to teach trades to people with no education. I was making a deal with the courts to get community service labor so I could repair houses for the elderly in the community and repair homes for single mothers and low income families. Aaron and I designed then I had invented a new kind of vaporizer that allowed you to inhale Pot or tobacco without any carcinogens that would basically prevent cancer from smoking. I had two gas models and three electric models. Once again I was taking over my world and I was on top of my game. That is when the shit hit the fan once more.

Chapter Six
Marshall Law Speed Trap

This is the actual letter that I wrote to the Judge, Police Chief, and Captain of the Bryan DPS after I happened in to a Speed trap.

On the night of 4/14/2011 at Approximately 0130 Hrs I was traveling south bound on SH 6 Traveling from Jerrell, Texas in rout to 4207 Woodcrest, Bryan Texas my place of residence. I had traveled to Miss Annie's house at the request of a friend because a contractor had stolen approx $ 12,000. From an elderly lady and I was asked to give a construction analysis and do the much needed repairs at no cost to the Lady.
I was traveling at a sustained rate of 60 miles per hour as indicated by my speedometer in my black 1993 Ford F150. In the clear night sky I could see a State Trooper's LED Lights on the right hand side of the road from about a mile and a half away so I started to decelerate. I knew that I was approaching a town so I looked for a radar sign or a Orange reduced speed ahead sign. There were none. Then I saw on the left hand side of the road a fifty miles per hour sign (that was gone when I returned) and behind it a black and white patrol car hiding in obscurity. As a soldier I immediately realized that this was an ambush (speed trap) and I started to pull over before the officer even turned on his lights and pulled out. The first thing that I noticed was that the DPS on the right was in front of a Champaign colored step side pickup with aluminum wheels which is not S.O.P for officers (rear end collisions). I pulled in front of Officer Cox squad car and put both of my hands outside the window as if I were a captive officer in a hostile environment and awaited the arrival of officer Lightfoot who was still turning around. When Officer Lightfoot approached my vehicle I gave him my name rank and business and told him that the only way that I could get my Insurance and registration was if he would allow me to get out of the truck and go to the other side because the glove box was obstructed. He allowed me to do so. After I gave him the information I walked to the center of the back of my truck between the patrol cars (violation of S.O.P. for rear end collision) and assumed the position of parade rest until the time that I was released from custody.
After reviewing my spotless driving and criminal record Officer Lightfoot said that I was a liar, that Jerrell was not as far as I said it was and that he was going to get to the bottom of this and started taking everything out of mu truck. He responded in glee when he retrieved my one gallon jug of communion wine that was located in the far right floor board and was completely inaccessible. He " what do we have hear" I asked for a field sobriety test and was denied, I asked for a breath test and was denied, I asked for a blood test and was denied.
Then he said "let's see what else we can find" and began removing the hundreds of items that volunteers had put in my truck as donations to my ministry.
Officer Cox of the DPS stood beside me and watched but he never spoke a word.
Officer Cox was squared away and treated me with the respect of my office. He also bore the cross of my savior proudly displayed on his uniform.
Officer Lightfoot with the swagger of a drunken brawler then magically appeared with a one inch glass jelly jar that contained a small amount of Green vegetated biomaterial that he claimed was Cannabis Sativa and placed it on the bed of my truck

in plain view of Officer Cox patrol video. He had no gloves on, he took no pictures, there were no fingerprints, there was no lab sample, and he never opened the Jar. Officer Lightfoot made railing accusations against me and accused me of being a dope head. When I was asked why a pastor would have pot in his truck I responder Verbatim "Sir possession of Cannabis Sativa is illegal in Texas but if I had any it would be because I have Bi Polar Disorder and cannabis sativa contains delta 9 tetrahydrocanabinol and is a serotonin inhibitor that blocks nuerotransmision and prevents mania but that is not my pot". Officer Cox then asked me if I had smoked any marijuana and I responded "Sir I have no pipe, I have no Bong, I have no papers and I have no lighter but I guess that I could eat it. Officer Cox smiled.

Officer Lightfoot then explained to me that he would take the pot and not report it and would just give me a drug paraphernalia charge. (For an empty jelly jar?) He then proceeded to tell me that he was giving me a ticket for open container because the bottle was within arm's reach. (Absolutely impossible).

Officer Cox finally spoke to me and said "We have given you lots of information and I want for you to answer one for me" "If you are what you say you are why you do bare tattoos and what do they represent"

I said thank you officer I will respond the best way I know how.

I have eighteen large red ants that go from my ankle to my belly button and it's a joke to make people laugh and draw them to me. (It is a reminder that when it's all done I will be an ant bed). Next on my right forearm I bare an angiogram of the words Life and Death which represent that although I may appear as death I am really Light. I then told him that on my right shoulder I bore the banner of a US Army soldier over the unit crest of a 13 Foxtrot because I am a forward observer. (a fist with a lightning bolt representing God's judgment on the wicked after the ancient order of Saint Barbara). I then told him that below that was an image of seven different guitars representing the fact that I was a master guitar player and I used my talent to draw men to me. I then directed Officer Cox to my left forearm which bears a yellow warning sign with a curvy road on it to remind us that there would be dangerous roads ahead and that we should proceed with caution. On my left shoulder I bare the names of my children and another guitar. (Sorry no cool meaning this time) I asked them if they would like for me to remove my shirt and show them my last tattoo and they complied. I removed my shirt exposing another angiogram located between my shoulder blades and I said "I bare the mark of the illuminati diamond, it represents the four elements of science and it is my heritage because I am the son of a Mason that is the son of a Mason dating all the way back to the knights Templar and that I was a Master Mason.

Officer Lightfoot rudely told me to put my shirt back on. I was completely courteous and respectful and I did not understand why officer Lightfoot was angry with me or why he treated my office as a public servant with such disrespect. He must hate Pastors.

Officer Lightfoot then handed me quite possibly the most inaccurate ticket ever created and explained to me that he still didn't know what was really up but that he was going to let me off easy and not charge me with the pot (which was not mine and disappeared as quickly as it had magically appeared in the first place) but that I would receive a drug paraphernalia charge and an open container charge because my wine bottle (a pastors communion wine) was within arm's reach (aprox. six feet away). I thanked him for his time and asked him if the exemption of the drug paraphernalia law didn't state that if I manufactured smoking products I could have them with me during the course of my business and Officer Lightfoot told me " If seek any course of action against this ticket I will personally seek vengeance upon you and I will put you in jail at any time in the next two years and that every person that was ever caught with pot in his town would be immediately arrested (The Law) and that it would be my fault". I thanked him for squaring me away, took my ticket and got the heck out of there as soon as I could.

Both squad cars should have video and audio

(but you won't find lightfoot's)

Now my professional analysis of the officers as a Pastor, Teacher, counselor, and a Senior Drill instructor's personal assistant at the FATC at Fort Sill follows.

Officer Cox is squared away. The only deficiency in his dress and appearance was a cross proudly displayed on his uniform (violation of dress code). He was courteous, respectful and professional and respected the public office that I held.

Officer Lightfoot is what we soldiers call a dirt bag. His footwear was not spit shined, his uniform was not well kept, His candor was that of a bar room brawler, he was disrespectful to my public office, He called me a liar, If I did have pot I should have been arrested on the spot and if I did not have pot then how could an empty jelly jar be drug paraphernalia. By my observations he cannot write, he cannot spell, he does not know where he is at, he does not know the speed limit, he cannot tell time, he cannot tell the difference between solid black and grey in fact he cannot even spell grey (GRAY), he cannot dictate information properly (1796 Ford ?). He cannot judge height, he does not know direction. He does not know Texas law, and he does not know his job.

In Summery I feel that officer Lightfoot is a complete disgrace to his uniform and all of the fine men and women that serve as law enforcement officers. I feel that he should be suspended without pay until a complete internal investigation has occurred and after due process of law I hope that he is permanently disbarred from law enforcement forever.

With all due respect

Rev. Nathon Quinn Dees

CEO and Founder Three Dees Associates

The Next day Aaron and I went back to Investigate and the Sherriff in Franklin told us "You will not find the Truth that you seek here, You must look elsewhere" and I saw that he bore the Square and Compass and I said "Thank you Brother" and left as fast as my Old Ford Betsy could move and drove straight to the DPS Headquarters.

I had been asked to go pick up a motorcycle for a friend and I was driving across Texas to get it when I started having highway hypnoses in the middle of the day for no apparent reason. I was passing out while I was driving during the middle of the day for no apparent reason. I was drinking energy drinks to try and stay awake and slamming coffee. Nothing seemed to help. Finally I pulled over at a convenience store and I heard the words diabetic coma in my head so I went in and bought a gallon of distilled water and some jalapeño peppers to counter act the effects of what was happening to me. I went outside and walked to the back of the store where I forced myself to throw up. I regurgitated almost strait sugar from all of the energy drinks and my body was shutting down. I walked up and down the drive way for nearly an hour before I had stabilized my condition enough to drive again. I then proceeded to the grocery store where I went to the pharmacy and explained to the pharmacist that I was a former combat lifesaver medic from the Army and what conditions I was treating myself for and I bought enough over the counter medicine to save my own life. I called the paramedics and they arrived nearly forty five minutes later. They checked all of my vitals and explained to me that I basically knew more about what was happening to me that they did and that there was really nothing more that they could do for me so the y released me and I went on my way. I made it to Austin where I got my friend Matt Cool to drive me back home to Bryan where I would seek help to find out what was really happening to me the next day. The following morning Aaron left for Austin to take Matt back home and I went to get some help for my condition.

I wanted a pet scan to check the levels of serotonin in my brain because I thought that I has Serotonin Toxicity Syndrome so I contacted the University first so that I could get a referral to the local MHMR where I could get sent to a hospital for the PET scan at no cost to me since there was no VA facility in Bryan.

Chapter Seven
Government Sanitarium from Hell

This was a big mistake. The girl at A&M that I talked to had been my councilor before and was another cookie cutter psychologist so when I described to her in great detail what had happened to me and why I was there she basically betrayed me and sold me out. She sent a letter to the MHMR that said I was confused and having troubling thoughts which was a complete and total lie so when I arrived for help I was met with a level of opposition that I would have never expected in a million years. Since I was a U.S. Army veteran and had mental illness they assessed that I was a danger to myself and to society. Since they did not know who I was they thought that I was delusional when I told them that I was a former pastor and that I owned a business. They did not believe anything that I said because I was a mental patient. I had been sent to school by the VA to receive training to become a peer support specialist for the mentally ill and I was actually a councilor at the VA working as a mediator between the doctors and patients. I had been in college studying psychology and had authored a book on mental illness and I was a thirteen foxtrot U.S. Army veteran that had received combat lifesaver training as a medic and I had completed water utility safety school at Texas A&M.

Everything that I told them was completely true and accurate but they did not care. They did not check out my story. They did not call my doctor. They arrested me against my will and sent me to a CIA maximum security psycho ward on the sixth floor of the Michael DeBakey VA Hospital in Houston and I was now a prisoner. Hell, I thought that I was going to the hospital for a pet scan I had no Idea that I was being arrested. I went in for help. I was articulate, calm, I knew exactly what I was talking about and I had proof of everything that I had said but no one wanted to hear what I had to say.

I was some U.S. Army violent psycho that needed to be incarcerated because I was dangerous. This was my reward for a life of service to my country and community. I had no arrest record, I had never been in a fight and I had spent my whole life in servitude to the church, my country, and my community and I was doing it again.

I was under contract to buy a church and start a school, not hurt other people or myself but that is not the way that they saw me. I was manic. I was dangerous. I was out of control. I was delusional. Well it turns out that I must have been completely delusional for ever asking anyone for help in the first place because the cause and effect of going to doctors for help completely destroyed my life and left me homeless and broke.

Chapter Eight
No Honor for Heroes

When I arrived at the hospital I was arrested, stripped of everything that I owned and confined to a cell. I didn't understand what was going on yet and I did not know why they just didn't give me an x ray and send me home. No one ever checked me or treated me for the condition that had nearly cost me my life and since it was on a Friday I would not even see a real doctor until the following Monday. It took until one AM before they finally in processed me and took me to my quarters. By this time I had realized what was going on and I had asked for a pen and paper to start taking notes so I could document what was being done to me.

So two days before I was free and I owned a business and I was an inventor and now I was a ward of the state under supervision for suicide and homicide and they were trying to force me to take meds against my will when I had been off of them for over a year under my doctors care. I was in complete recovery and I was a peer support technician that actually worked for the VA as a volunteer in Austin but here in Houston where they would not even call my doctor or check my records or anything.

They had miss diagnosed me and prescribed me meds after five minutes of interview. I told them that I was a holistic practitioner and that I used herbal medication and diet to control my condition and that in fact the two medicines that they had prescribed for me were not for the illness that I had and that they would counter act each other and endanger my life. It said it right on the drug information pamphlet that came with the medicine. The nurses said that if the prescriptions were wrong that you needed to tell the doctor, well I had not even seen a real doctor yet and they were trying to force me to take the wrong meds against my will. I felt as if this were some kind of weird conspiracy and that they were trying to kill me. I did what I was trained to do. I established my rank and position and set up a chain of command.

I found out who was the highest ranking soldier in the psycho ward and who was most capable of taking command of the situation. It was me once again. I was the only one that refused to take the crazy pills and I was the only one there that had not actually done anything wrong to myself or anyone else to get there. I was the only one that new the time and date and where I was and why I was there every one else was so drugged up that they did not know what was going on. Now that I was a pastor that basically gave me a commission and made me a chaplain so I posted my name, rank and position outside my door and I let them know that I was freemason. The next morning people had started writing their name and rank on my door so I could identify the people that were still sane and knew what was going on.

The next morning at chow I was directed to the officers table where I was briefed by a man named Kenny Roberts that said he was a three star general.

Hell, this was a psycho ward this guy could have been anyone but we had been stripped of all of our personal belongings and jewelry and shoes and everything when we were admitted and Kenny was wearing a two hundred fifty dollar Adidas jogging suit, Reeboks and a Rolex watch.

Kenny told me that everything was going to be alright and that I was not going to get out anytime soon or for at least seventy two hours and that I should just relax and make the best of it. So that Saturday morning I was seated at the officers table with a three star General on the sixth floor maximum security government controlled military psych ward because less than forty eight hours before I was dying on the side of the road, saved my own life and then went to a doctor to get an X-ray.

Chapter Nine
Hell on Earth

How could this possibly be happening to me? What did I do? Who did I piss off? Why was this happening to me?!

Ok so here is the score, It is Saturday morning, I am locked up in a maximum security military psycho ward, I can't see a doctor until Monday. They are trying to force me to take medication that I don't want and don't need. It's the week end so they cannot and will not call my real doctor Dr. Clayton. I haven't been in the military for over fourteen years and I'm in here with guys that just came off the front line in the Middle East with fucking bullet holes in their head that are completely whacked out. I am still very ill from whatever sickness that I had that got me here in the first place and no one will treat me for it. Alright Nathon, we have been in some fucked up situations before and I saw one flew over the koo koo's nest before so I know the game, let's play ball.

I asked for a felt tipped marker and some paper (You could not have a pen because you might kill someone with it) and I started taking notes and writing down everything that was happening to me and everyone else. Well that made me dangerous to them and pissed everyone off. So the fun began. I started interviewing everyone in there that I could actually hold a conversation with and helping out all the war heroes and combat veterans that were locked up for serving their country. Everyone knew who I was by noon chow and the lines were drawn. As always you either love Nathon or hate Nathon so I had basically divided the room into two camps. Those that were used to being railroaded by the system were telling me just to shut up and take the meds so that we could all get out and every one that understood what was happening were supporting me and telling me their own horror stories about this place.

I had a Navy seal that wanted to kill me, my roommate of course. There were Delta force Marines, Army Rangers, Navy Seals and elite Navy rescue guys. These people were hard core they had PTSD, Bi Polar disorder, Schizophrenia, drug and alcohol problems, suicidal tendencies, and not to mention homicidal tendencies. Hell, some of them were just getting a break from killing people on the front line in the Middle East. This was definitely not the local MHMR.

The place looked clean at first glance but by the time that you took a good look you could tell that things were unkept and unsanitary. They only cleaned the day room every couple of days and there was food all stuck to the tables and floors, the sinks didn't work in half of the rooms, and they were rewashing and reusing disposable plastic silverware. All of the linins smelt like septic like they were washed in waste water or something but they were definitely not clean. Most of all the war heroes and men and women that had lost their sanity serving their country and were scarred for life had fewer rights than a TDC prison inmate. You could not go outside, you could not take a walk, you could not do exercise or PT, there was no smoking, no newspapers, no decent reading material and if you so much as looked at a staff member wrong they would medicate you against your will and put you in a holding cell. There were E8 US Navy master chiefs scrubbing the floors and cleaning windows. This place was a disgrace and a dishonor to the fine men and women that had served our country. I have actually been in jails in third world countries that were better that the sixth floor of the Houston VA sixth floor maximum security psycho ward. Most of all we were being held prisoner for crimes that we did not commit.

When it came time to shave you stood in a line with the people that were allowed to shave and one at a time under supervision you were given one of those blue disposable open faced body razors that they use for surgery. Not even a safety razor. They were so bad that we had contest to see who could actually shave without cutting your face. Some of the guys looked like hamburger meat when they got through. I almost won the shaving contest once but a female sergeant found one speck of blood on my face and I got beat by a marine. We were the only ones that were not bleeding profusely. One of the saddest moments for me was watching the red blood of a U.S. Marine pour down his face into the sink while he tried to shave with this surgical ball razor. What a fucking dishonor, what a fucking disgrace. Some of the men were completely incoherent and just shuffled up and down the hall completely whacked out of their minds on psych drugs others were under guard and not allowed to leave their rooms. They were more or less there permanently and that was their goal for me. To fuck me up on meds bad enough so that I would become incoherent and they could keep me there forever. It was not going to happen to me. Fuck them. I refused to take the meds and I refused to even where my ID or arm band. The first thing that I noticed when they put the arm band on me was that it had my whole social security number printed on it in large bold print. I ripped it off and told them that they were fucking crazy if they thought that they could publicly display my social security number on my arm and that it was a violation of HIPA, the freedom of information act and it violated my civil rights as an American. They said well you can't have your meds unless you have an arm band and I told them they could stick them up their ass with their fucking arm band because I was not going to take their poison and I was not going to wear the arm band when my social security number was on it. Everyone saw my defiance and realized that they had a choice too and started refusing the wrong medications and asking for a doctor to review their cases. I was causing them way more trouble than I was worth. By shift change and evening chow I had already turned the place upside down and everyone there knew who I was. I was still seated at the officers table with Crazy Kenny the three star general and I had started giving away all of my food. I don't drink milk so I gave it away, I don't eat deserts so I gave it away, I don't eat white bread so I gave it away and I don't eat sugar so I gave it away. In fact there was very little nutritional value in any of the meals they were serving and the food sucked so I started giving mine away to everyone else. It was like an auction. "Hey Dees what do you want to get rid of" well I don't eat this and I don't like that and this has no nutritional value hell take it all I could use a fast for a couple of days. By the time I left I had everyone in the day room sharing their food and giving up what they did not need.

It was almost as if I reminded them that we were all soldiers and that we were all in this together and that we had to stick together and pull our resources in order to survive.

That day after chow it happened. We were sitting at the table when Crazy Kenny who was at least six foot four and had curly flaming red hair with blue eyes started singing Beatles songs at random. Well it was on. He started drumming on the table and we started singing every classic rock song that we knew for hours but Kenny loved the Beatles and we sang them nearly every time we got together after that. One day we busted out a Beatles song in the middle of the hall way right in front of the nurses' station and did it so bad ass that when we finished the guards stopped what they were doing and came and listened. One of them even shook my hand afterward and told that I was great. Kenny would do the Paul McCartney parts and I would be John Lennon and our harmonies were pretty good. We were both singers and professional musicians that had played in bands and sang for years so we really enjoyed singing in the nut house.

Chapter Ten
Meeting Dr. Do Little

Finally I get assigned to the head psychiatrist Dr. Hartly Little. When he interviewed me he asked what my trade was. I told him that I was a Master Mason, Master Craftsman and that I knew all commercial and residential trades. He wrote " Mr. Dees is obviously delusional and thinks that he can do anything" I told him that I had the license to prove everything that I said and that in fact I had more license than his whole staff. Here is the problem Dr. Little. You spent your whole life and all of your daddy's money to learn one trade and you have about a 120 IQ and can only do one thing. I have a GED and I can do anything and I have around 160 IQ and it pisses you off. "Mr. Dees has severe Axis two Narcissistic Personality Disorder and I recommend that he be permanently institutionalized by the State of Texas". I said you want to put me in the state home!
That is very Funny Dr. Do Little because Ron Pfiser the head of the Peer Support program tried to hire me to work there at the recommendation of Dr Clayton at the Austin VA and I am a licensed Peer Support Specialist dumbass!

 Well after that he made some calls and actually talked to Dr. Clayton that confirmed to him that everything that I had told him was the truth and that I had been under her care and worked at the VA for NAMI and that I was a genius and perfectly fine and that she had me off of the meds. Realizing that he was in a completely fucked up situation he found a loop hole. Since he did not know the special circumstances that the Army gave me for discharge, when he saw that I only had 18 months of active duty service he yanked all of my VA benefits and billed me $ 15,000.00 for a six day stay against my will. Then he filled on social security to garnish my Government check to pay the VA back for six days of hell under involuntary incarceration and threw me out in the street to be homeless and broke and destroy my life.

Chapter Eleven
WTF Could Possibly Happen Next?

Aaron had taken all of our most valuable possessions, like my 74 Stratocaster, My father's 1914 Silver Anniversary H.N. White trumpet, my Marshall amps and my George Snydo Original Print and put them in the Pawn shop for safe keeping and get some gas money to come get me from Houston where Dr. Little had just thrown me out onto the street. This turned out to be very wise because by the time that we got back to College Station our house had been broke into three times, Guy had moved out and took all of his shit and moved into a FEMA trailer, Chris had stole my electronic Drum Set and filled false charges on me and Aaron claiming the equipment was his and their friend the Land Lord had given me a fake city eviction order and filled false charges on me. Guy's friend Nathan Winchester who was my old land Lord that I had done some work for filled false breaking and entering charges against me and Guy's friend Justin Murphy filled false Kidnapping charges on me because his daughter ran away and was hiding in the woods and I had absolutely nothing to do with any of this. Some other College Kids from A&M had stole my CNC machine prototype and all of Aaron's video games, filled false charges claiming the stuff was his and my ex wife Athea had filed restraining orders against me and it had been a Year since I even saw her and she lived 150 miles away and my two step sons never spoke to me again. Nearly every family member had blocked me and unfriended me and changed their e mails and phone numbers and my best friends rejected me and shut Aaron and I out.

The only person in College Station that would even talk to me or shake my hand was Bill Allen from the Harry Bikers TV show, on the History Channel, who was a friend of mine.

Bill looked me strait in the eye and told me that the only thing that I had done wrong was be different and that I needed to get out of town immediately. We said a short prayer and I left. Chris Text Aaron and told us that there was an APB to arrest both of us on site if we came anywhere near Texas A&M. I was brought in for questioning three times of the next few days and by the time that I finally had a detective look at everything he was absolutely amazed to learn that there was absolutely no evidence to any of the charges and that I had been the victim of a highly elaborate plot by my friends and suggested that I leave College Station ASAP so I did.
Who would have thought that Texas A&M and College Station were the CIA New World Order Headquarters for Monsanto and Homeland security Marshall law Civil Terrorism training.

We ended up living in a gutted abandoned trailer house at my friends Tim Butler's house in Houston. Before we could get settled or regroup there the trailer was broken into and my Marshall amps and the rest of my tools were stolen so we packed up the few things that we had left and headed for Austin. When we got to Austin my friend Sean Pollard let us move in the Barn in his back yard in exchange for working on it and Aaron and I started to rebuild once more with absolutely nothing.

Chapter Twelve
Then Things got even Weirder
As if that was even possible

I had done some jobs for Sean and made some money, my Buddy Jimmy down the street let me rent his house with no money down if I remodeled it for him so Aaron and I got our own place and he got a job and we started over again. Something was happening to me and my perceptions and understanding of this great conspiracy were all coming to light. I was doing much research about ten hours a day reading about ascension and the pineal gland and crystals and holistic healing. I learned about Chakras and meditation from my friend Summer Walters. I learned about the Book of Enki and the writings of Zecheria Sitchen. I read the Emerald Tables of Thoth and Hermes Thrise Greate, I learned the virtues of Pathogarus, The Gnostic Gospels from the Nag Hammad library. I learned about Nassim Harameim and sacred geometry. I built a pyramid in my back yard out of tube steel and started harnessing zero point energy. I was on fire again.

I was meditating at my desk and the voice spoke to me and told me to go treasure hunting so I went out prospecting in the creek. While down in the creek bed looking for signs of place gold I heard " Find the Ore Find the gold" and as soon as I heard that is looked down and picked up a strange piece of brown ore and took it home to research it. Well, It turns out that I had moved into the Strewn field of the Comet that hit the Gulf Coast sixty million years before and killed the dinosaurs. I found 120 lbs of the rarest Stony Iron Achondrite meteorite. They passed every test and they were radioactive, non magnetic, non conductive, and were 94% pure iron crystal carbonate black diamond inside with fusion crust and Regmaglyphs outside. Regular stony Iron sold for $50 a gram on the internet and some HED Achondrites were up to $500 a gram meaning that I had just found around Two and a half million dollars worth of meteorites.

Chapter Thirteen
Cock blocked Again

My friend had Just Got his P.E. degree from the University of Texas and worked for the State Department of Transportation as an engineer. He and his colleagues from work proved my theory and verified that they were meteorites for me but could not offer me the proper validation that I needed to make a sell. Another is a machinist and welder and his father is a Professor of metallurgy and we all knew that they were meteorites but not a single University or museum would validate my find even though they could not prove that I was not right. This one asshole at the North Texas State observatory could not debunk me and when he exposed it to the Geiger counter to prove that it was not radioactive and the Geiger counter went off he said "Well this is an old Geiger counter and it is probably malfunctioning". I told him that he was full of shit and explained to him how that a Geiger counter was nothing more than an anode with a speaker and an analog current transformer and that he was a fucking idiot. Then he tried to tell me that it was hematite and I told him that hematite had a melting point of 1500 Degrees Fahrenheit and I whipped out my mini torch and showed them that it just started getting red at 2000 degrees F. Three Museums and three Universities and everyone that I talked to knew less about meteorites than I did. I was so pissed off over this. My P.E. friend took his information and samples and went to the McDonald observatory in West Texas as an academic and asked them point blank if this whole meteorite thing was a scam to control the market. The man looked at my friends hand and saw the square and Compass. The answer was Yes. They told him that since no one can actually swear that something is a meteorite unless it is a documented fall of a typical known type and that the Scammers like the Meteorite Men Show were there to create a false market for the commodities and only validate the ones that they or their colleagues found.

Chapter Fourteen
Enough is Enough

In addition to the Stony Irons I had identified at least six different other meteorites in the creek and collected them as well as Crystallized Calcite Alomasaurus teeth, Megalodon teeth. I also found Precifincterus fossils in the same creek proving that my theory about the source of the meteors was correct. All of the normal people were getting angry with me and were mad because I had discovered these things and no one but the few smart people that I knew understood that I was right and I lost several good friends over this. They would actually say that I was too smart to believe this and that it was embarrassing them to see me this way so I told them to get the Fuck out of my house.
 Nearly every single person that I knew in Austin was hooked on Smoking Methamphetamines, Shooting Meth, or taking Adoral.

 They all were suffering from Meth induced Schizophrenia and their ego identities would attack me at random and I was understanding the great negative forces that had been set against me here because I was in Fact a chosen one and an RH negative hybrid from a royal knights Templar blood line. It all started making since to me.

 I was the reincarnation of an Ascended Master. My First name is from AkhenNaton "The son of Aton" and In Ancient Hebrew Nathon means a continual giving gift of God. My middle name is Quinn which is Gaelic for intelligence and Royalty under refuge and Dees is Scottish and means Descendants of King David from the Davidson clan. I am from the CulDees of Iona Scotland and I had no idea about any of this before. When I studied the CulDees I found that they taught and believed the same exact principals and theory that I had developed on my own called the "Quaternary". In fact the Tattoo of the illuminate diamond on my back was an ancient symbol of my clan representing the four elements of science. CulDees is from Chaldeans and means Worshipers of God. I was the incarnation of an ancient astronomer priest from a clan of Masonic Warrior monks.

Chapter Fifteen
Good by New World Order
Hola Costa Rica
Tuanis Pura Vida

As soon as my lease was up I gave away all of my equipment. I Left some stuff with my sister, Packed up every single rock, stone, meteorite and fossil then drove to Florida to find my brother Damon who had been clean and sober and on his own now for seven years since he was deported from Costa Rica. I put all of my treasures in a secret location in Miami and I flew back to Jaco, Costa Rica to live with and care for my father who was now blind.
I gave Damon my Ford truck and my tools so that he could provide for himself and Pop and I flew home back to where I felt safe and Aaron would follow us shortly. When I got to Jaco my friend Mr. Woods that owned my Hostel building had a house that had been damaged by thieves and left vacant so I remodeled it completely in two weeks and did such a good job that Floyd told me that he intended to hold the real estate for ten more years and that I could have the house to live in for free until we decided to sell the property.

 All I know is that I was home and that I had no intentions what so ever of ever returning to the Unites States of Confusion. I was Home and Byron and I were so happy to have escaped from the American New World Order Death machine. There were many more adventures ahead for me in Costa Rica and I was ready to finish my ascension and enter into my Shamnistic role as an El Elehido "Chosen one" and a Reike healer.

By this time I was so in tune with my inner dialog that I was discovering new things almost daily.

I found ten different types of semi precious minerals that wash up on the beach at random on certain days.

I collect hundreds of pounds of Chalcedony Crystal quartz, celestial quartz, Agate, Smokey Quartz, Rose Quartz, Amber Quartz, Heliotrope Bloodstone and fossilized Dinosaur poop.

It's like, I'm the only person that ever even noticed them all over the beach. It's like treasure hunting every day. I had discovered ley lines with my dowsing rods and the energies here were off the scale so I built a new pyramid and set 120 lbs of Quartz in it in the shape of a pyramid and then put meteorites on the top and it started creating so much power that my body literally jolts when I touch it and It ignites my Chakras and my appendages all start vibrating as my crown and Third eye Chakras open up and my Pineal gland starts producing DMT.

I had started my next incarnated manifestation as

"The Guru AkhNathon "An Ascended Master and teacher of higher consciousness.

The Illuminutty

New World Disorder

Ok so I survived Book one and Book Two and now I'm back in Costa Rica safe and sound as an intellectual refuge. I have managed to clear my mind and focus more clearly on my future. Through introspection and self evaluation I was able to see through the bad programming and come to a higher revelation of the truth. Lies and misconceptions had been taught to me in American society as Gospel truths my entire life. When these concepts of the constructs of reality were met with certain realisms they caused Cognitive Dissonance with the primary operating psychological program and shorted me out. It is like putting a person in a round room and telling them to sit in the corner.

It was no longer a Matter of Belief but more of a matter of understanding and Gnosis through higher Consciousness. I had to lay out every construct of my primary operating command in such a way as to monitor the cause and effect of each primary beliefs function and end result. After doing so and reorganizing my belief system by inventorying and evaluating clearly the things that I CHOSE to believe I was able to break free from the Ego identity that had been created by Religion and Society in the United States of Confusion.

Chapter One

Video Gaming Theory

My son Aaron and my daughter Natolie are both Gamers and as a Father I have spent countless hours watching them kill aliens, save planets, overtake war zones in alternate realities and learn to overcome obstacles and achieve Mastery. I have an application theory that I call "Mastery Application" everyone is always recreating the wheel. Once you achieve mastery in one art you immediately apply that same exact level of expertise to every area of your life. So here is where the theory applies.

When one meditates on nothing and removes oneself from one's self you can then throw up your internal video monitor and evaluate who exactly is playing your avatar in this three Dimensional reality Game. Understand that in the format of an RPG you constantly check your health, Your Spells, Your Knowledge, and you inventory what you truly need to accomplish your task. You would never knowingly nor willingly choose destructive actions that would be detrimental to the success of the mission or subtract from you overall performance and placement ranking. So why then in Life are we Complete Fucktards that have absolutely no Fucking idea what is going on when in an alternate holographic reality we are Gods!

So I'm like "Son, Life is coming against you and you are taking it pretty hard. You have made some incorrect decisions and you are suffering from the cause and effect of your decisions. You feel as if everything is against you and to every positive effort there is an equal and opposite effort against you. Well that's because it is!!!! In fact it is the Ebb and flow of Conscious reality and the very struggle to find balance within.

 So you are a Jedi Star Fleet Commander and a Four Star General in Knights of the New Republic and Medal of Honor but in the Third Dimensional Holographic Reality you are living on your friends couch and can't get a job because you have no car etc etc etc. This makes absolutely no Fucking sense at all. In fact it is almost impossible to believe. You see in the Military and Marshall arts when we recognize a Rank of another branch of Service or fighting style and we still honor their mastery and treat them as equals, well you young people can create a perfect world on a screen and can't tie your own shoes in reality and this is absolute insanity! You are not applying the Mastery that you have already achieved. "But that guy went to school for that" Big Fucking deal you mindless automaton, the guy that invented it DID NOT GO TO SCHOOL FOR IT, HE JUST DID IT!!!!!!GET IT! He just Did It!

My point is, if you can create and manipulate a perfect life for yourself on Simms then why does your real life suck? It is because you fail to apply the lessons that you have learned in the Video reality to the Functioning Reality. It's like saying "Oh I can't Drive a FORD I was only taught to drive a Chevy. I can't Play Bass I was only taught to play guitar. I can't fly a plane of surf or skate or shoot or skate board in real life I can only do it on a video game. I call Bullshit! If the basic skills needed to achieve a Task are present in a Video reality then they are present in the Functioning reality. It's the same Fucking Brain; it is the same Fucking Game!

The game is called "Evolutionary Ascension" and you are the Avatar. You are a three dimensional Psychotronic Humanoid Borg on a Planetary Omniversity and you must graduate or you will be recycled infinitely as an unascended gaming character in the Holographic matrix until you Wake up Evolve and Ascend. Unfortunately Your DNA has been modified and you have to unlock your condones to access your akasha records so you are Stupid and your Karma Score Card keeps following you from incarnation to incarnation until you get it right.

Wow I just explained the concept of cyclic reality in one paragraph. All of the Eastern, Middle East, Mesa American, Inuit, Gaelic, Pictic, Egyptian, Zoroaster, and on and on and on all the way back to ancient Samaria believed and practiced this Philosophy until the dawning of the age of Materialism and the Birth of Organized religion. Akhenaton was sent to destroy religion and bring truth, Hermes was sent to do it, Dioneses was sent to do it, Pythagoras was sent to do it, Horus was sent to do it, Krishna was sent to do it, Thoth was sent to do it, Enoch was sent to do it, Quetzucatal was sent to do it Yeshua "Jesus Christ" was sent to do it and now I had been incarnated in this Eon to do it again.

Chapter Two

Programmed on a Foundation of Lies

The problem with child rearing inside the American societal culture such as the one that I was raised in is a blurring of the truth while programming the foundations that the child lives on. When we don't clearly define what is fact, what is fiction, and what is faith so we establish a foundation of misinformation, half truths and Folklore. Santa Clause, The Easter Bunny, and Jesus all on the same plain of existence with Satan getting his own Holiday Halloween when he was in direct opposition to Jesus. Santa Clause and the Easter Bunny getting Billing over the Christ? Blowing the young and impressionable minds of children with Lies and Myths for the purpose of what? Propagating societal lies for fun? Teaching you children that it is OK to lie if it is tradition? Forcing the older children to lie to the younger children to further propagate more lies? This is absolute Fucking insanity and is not only Cruel to children but it establishes a standard of no moral absolutes in the name of celebrating moral absolutes and programs your children to believe in Historical mythical figures as Gods and Deities for the purpose of entertainment only to eventually learn that it was a lie but yet hold true to the religious iconic idolatry that the icons represent. This is where the foundation for theological cognitive dissonance is established.

I never once did any of this and I never lied to my children because it was popular. I explained clearly the difference between folk lore and much and I also explained to my children that the other parents lacked integrity and lie to their children but I did not want to do that. We had no Santa, we did not celebrate Halloween, and we never celebrated Easter. This made me a bad parent? I was protecting the integrity of the relationship that I had with my Kids as a source of accurate information and truth!

Chapter Three

The Book of N8

1. In the Beginning was the end and the end was the beginning thereof.

2 What is now was then and what was then will be now again in the Cyclic flow of consciousness.

3 The beginning is the end of that which was before it.

4 This is the Ubiquitous Flow of conscious Reality as you perceive it an ever evolving always improving program in a cosmic quest for completion only to perpetually reproduce for infinity.

5 A Holographic 3D Reality constructed and controlled by the sentient Conscious Observation of other Intelligible Humans in agreement.

6 A plastic shapeable reality that you can control to some extent by exercising ones will and determination to Rise Above the simplicity of Normality and Create a Better World to live in for the Whole by raising Awareness and Consciousness to the Masses instead of educational Mind Control in an Slave Society of mindless automatons.

Chapter Four

Pull Your Head Out

This is a definitive guide to pulling your head out of your ass and getting a clue.

First things first. Stop Bullshitting yourself! If you are fucked up you damn well know it so just stop lying to yourself and everyone else. Stop comparing yourself to other people that are more Fucked up than you are and Stop Blaming other people for you being Fucked up. Pinch, Wipe, Flush and Get over it.

Now that we have decided to get real and actually evaluate how and why we became Fucked up in the first place and correct the programming errors that brought us to this place.

Chapter Five

Troubleshooting 101

Self Diagnosis. Use introspection and some meditation to analyze your condition and answer your own questions intelligently and with objectivity like you actually have a clue and you know right from wrong because you do!

Stop playing dumb ass like some immature little kid that pretends to not know that wrong actions and wrong behavior lead to bad results. If you don't have a Clue Get One! Pull your fucking head out of your ass and find out what is right and wrong from some one that has their shit together at any level of life that is better than yours!

Start filing your mind with good information and stop hanging around with STUPID PEOPLE that do STUPID SHIT!

Separate yourself from STUPID PEOPLE that do STUPID THINGS and start hanging out with SMART PEOPLE that are doing POSSATIVE THINGS! So if you're at a Metal bar and your old friend says "Hey lets Smoke this Meth and Jump in the Mosh PITT" and your new friend looks at your like "WTF" go with the Smart Guy! You have just pulled your head out of

your ass and Got a Clue at that very moment and the Next
time you might get to be the Smart Friend!

Chapter Six

More Rambling

So is my Narcissism not the equal and opposite reaction to
your stupidity? Is there something wrong with me because I
can see what's wrong with everything? Why can't they see
the flaws in the constructs of the values of religion and
society? Why would a world of mindless automatons have a
say in the future of mankind or the planet? Why would it not
make perfect since to eliminate the week and feeble minded
so that the race can flourish? What kind of selfishness would
allow everyone to suffer because of the actions of the Dumb
Masses? Is this social, ethnic and religious cleansing not the
very hope of all religion? Only by eliminating the Bad seed
can the good seed flourish and there are simply too many
average or normal people to sustain and a purging and
cleansing is inevitable and unavoidable. Mankind is a fungus
to the Earth that has grown out of control and outlived its

usefulness to the good of the whole and nature itself will find balance one way or another.

This is just another cycle in the planets evolution and has taken place many times with many beings and cultures. The masking of truth to enslave the dumb Masses has reached its critical mass but the intrinsic thinking ability of the dumb masses is so low that they still cannot evaluate the truth that is now being presented because it violates the core of their educational and religious programming. One will never be able to grasp the reality of Truth while clinging to superstitions, myths and religious ideologies when met with the indisputable truth that their world as they know it is coming to an end. The sooner the Better!

CHAPTER 7

New World Disorder

So I'm researching and researching trying to figure something out that's concrete. I am now an expert as it were on Atlantis, Lumeria, Mu, Ancient Mesopotamia, Egypt, Samaria, Mesoamerica, etc etc. I've studied every ancient religious text that I could get my hands on searching for any higher truth or in fact any truth at all by this point. The one thing that I knew for sure was that there was a grand conspiracy of misinformation out there and truths were only found deep beyond the surface of things.

Meanwhile back in the present all of the things I'm learning about the past all tie into the present and center around two families or blood lines. A brother, a half brother and a sister. Over and over again. Different names same story, same time lines, same results. A power struggle between two opposing forces for the rule of Earth. Yet none of it was real. Everything was a type and everything was holistic in an ever occurring infinite spiral of realities. Every Star was a god and every element a spirit and it was all a master program of seven basic harmonic tones. Frequency resonance creating the perceptions of a three dimensional holographic reality held together only by sentient consciousness and consciousness was failing rapidly on this planet.

All of the evidences showed that an elite few were controlling the World to some extent but yet it had to be done. Everything looked as if they were preparing for alien invasion and genocide while at the same time everything that they were doing would be absolutely necessary for maintain control and preserving the balance of the planet.

Those that know, know and those that do not know do not know. All knowledge is transient and in the very fiber of your DNA. There is nothing that is not known. There is only that that has not yet been revealed or understood but there is no thing that has not yet been conceived already in the prime directive of the program.

It is our task or goal as it were to wake up in this lifetime and come to the reality of what truly is and find balance with ourselves that we may achieve personal evolution and overcome this three dimensional existence and move on to a higher dimensional plane. What is , is.

Back to the story at hand.

 The Zionist banksters and the and the Royal families "NATO" are preparing to take over the Earth it would seem by destroying all religion and religious groups and forming a one world government through marshal law and genocide. The whole thing was playing out like some bad Hollywood movie or a high tech video game. The U.S. had become a slave state with a puppet government controlled by the families. Those that were in power were going to exterminate the human cattle and start over. As evil and sinister as it all seemed it all made a great deal of since to me. To a higher dimensional being we would be no different than any other lower life form is to us. The same prejudices that we show and experience over our own opinions towards certain life would be expressed by any other life form than ourselves. A dog is a dog unless it's your dog.

If you did know what was going to happen and you had a chance of saving the best of the best you would do so. If you were in power and you truly understood the events to come and had the ability to survive and reconstruct by whatever means necessary then you would do so. It just makes since.

Compassion is not a necessary trait for a surviving species. The substandard human species created on this planet by mistake must be eliminated and the quarantine lifted off of this planet for cosmic equilibrium to be achieved. It is no different than bad seed in your garden or a mutt dog breeding with your prize show dog. The bad DNA must be eradicated for the survival of the overall race. Or let's put it this way. It's not going to survive anyway in a post apocalyptic world.

They had discovered a way for them to live forever as it were by using self replicating Nanotechnology and creating an advanced humanoid Borg that was one with artificial intelligence. They no longer needed humans to do their bidding for them on Earth so they were going to exterminate them. What they did not realize in their selfish quest for eternity was that what they were creating already existed and they were it. We are the program. We are the self replicating life form and the infinite knowledge is available to those of a pure heart. It is appointed unto a man to live and die ass all things have a cycle. Nature shall run its course and it will determine who survives. What is , is.

They have created their modern Tower of Babble and the Aeons and Archons will once again set all things in order.

Haughty and high minded art thou Oh man that would try and reach the heavens and dethrone The God's if it were possible.

Eternity is found within one's own heart. It is the Cosmic Bliss of Love and nothing else. Only The Arc of Love can bend light frequency into reality. True life is consciousness as to be unconscious is to be void of life in this third dimensional reality. Your only existence is that that is held within your own perceptions of reality in this holographic dream World. Don't believe anything just be, for what is, is and what is not is not. It is truly your own perception of what is that creates the constructs of your own personal reality. All that shall be shall be as it was in the beginning that it shall be again. The cycle must continue and evolution of the species must occur.

They had created an insane society of impossible constructs that enslaved people into a realm of cognitive dissonance. By reconstructing the harmonic grid to one of imbalance they could prevent true bliss and understanding thereby preventing the masses to ever achieve inner peace or higher revelation. Feeding off of the suffering of the masses while they obtain great hordes of wealth for themselves until the time of the harvest just like cattle farmers fattening up a herd for slaughter. It was dinner time and their god's were returning to Earth for the harvest one more time.

So would end another cycle and a new and better world would begin.

It all seemed to have the same ending no matter how it played out. It would be a new beginning for someone, one way or another. There must be an end for a beginning to occur in every construct of reality.

Chapter 8

Comet ISON and the Great Deception

It is Oct of 2013 and as the Comet ISON quickly approaches Earth the U.S. Government has shut down in an effort to destroy the economy and declare Marshall Law on the People of the United States. FEMA region three is prepared for lock down and the East Coast is getting hit with fireballs daily now. All of the Government websites have been shut down including NASA and there is no information about any of this on the news. ISON already arced electrically with Mars and caused it to have a Coma and go Comet and everyone on the Earth is just too fucking stupid to realize the truth of what was really going on. Fukushima Japan is a fucking nuclear disaster and Cyclones were distributing radiation all over the world. Solar flares are increasing daily and the power grid on Earth would be knocked out any day now. You can almost time the solar flares and the Earth quakes that follow daily now. The great change is upon us and a New World Order is eminent but the one question still remained, who would be in control. I am predicting the return of the God's and the Judgment of the leaders of the Earth followed by a Millennium of peace on Earth. Let's just sit back and see what really happens.

As for me I will choose to be happy. N8

Aeons, Archons,

And

Escaping the

New World Disorder

By

Nathon Dees

So let's get strait to it.

The Planet Earth is under siege by a Hostile clan of Archon demigods called the Demiurge from the planet Saturn that use humans as slaves through mind control and thought manipulation using a harmonic grid network that causes disharmony of the primary Earth Matrix and Human DNA.

The sinister little bastards have been milking this planet and its resources for quite some time now and the stupid humans just line up to worship them like sheep being led to a slaughter.

Chapter One

The Human Obedience School

So since we know that the prime creator must ultimately have overriding control over the gaming matrix, then we can see that by building in a primordial race of utilitarian programmer beings and then forcing them to baby set a lower life form that would eventually supersede them creates a malevolent Task master.

Heck the whole solar system looks down on Humans and why not. They were created in the image of the prime creator and then given a paradise to destroy. Selfish, Self willed, Self Serving, indignant little brats with no respect for the balance of life. It's no wonder that the Earth itself kills them all off from time to time. Even Jesus was a Sheep herder and not a leader of men. He taught parables because people were simply too darn stupid to understand the simplicity of the message.

"Save Your Self"

We can think of the Archons as invisible wardens on a prison planet for the rehabilitation of contaminated souls that must be purified by evolving through an experience of human suffering on Earth. Proctors in a testing Matrix with your very souls' existence on the line, forever recycling until you break the cycle of Karma and ascend from the physical state Humanity into a higher frequency being of light energy.

Aeon, Archon, Demon, Angel, Demiurge, Deity, are all just archetypes for polar opposites in the control program. It is necessary for humans to have a visualization of something for them to comprehend it. So then all of the archetypes become beautiful Angels and ugly Demons and sources of power, wisdom, or energy become Gods. Spirituality itself is the main identifier of a un evolved soul that lacks understanding in the first place. All is energy, all is science, and everything can be explained. There is always a way to explain everything but that doesn't mean that you will understand it and that is where your dumb avatars, parables and visualizations come in so that you can understand the constructs of these mechanisms.

Chapter Two

Delusional Precepts

Of the false Reality

A belief is defined as a pneumatological activity, maintaining a psychological state in which an individual holds a conjecture or premise to be true. Dispositional and occurrent belief concerns the contextual activation of the belief into thoughts (reactive of propositions) or ideas (based on the beliefs premise).

Well just because you hold an idea to be true does not by any means make it true without uncontroversial scientific proof. Without this all you have done is based the foundation of your reality on Dogmatic idealism and popular consensus of theory.

The Kybalion clearly states as comic law that all truths are half truths and my own teachings dictate that all truths are only relevant to the depth of the belief of the believer. Objective reality constricted only by your limitations of practical probability and possibility or even worse, a false reality based on unrealistic fantasy creations of the human imagination.

If your foundational operating system is based purely on belief, then you have a cracked slab with no integrity that you "Hope" with no real personal evidential data that your unfounded dogmatic belief is true and real. Then to add to the problem you add emotion and ego identity to the mix solidifying the creation of the religious false self holding the true self captive in a cell of lies and misinformation.

This quasi religious reality is maintained through ritualistic practice of subservience through fear and need for acceptance both by religious society and the Deity Avatar iconic representation itself.

It was never necessary for you to believe anything in the first place. When you come to an understanding on your own you very seldom fill in the blanks with belief, understanding full well that all you have developed is a probable theory and nothing more. Betting eternity on a hunch based on someone else's beliefs without personal Gnosis based on valid historical data and understanding is just short of industrial Strength Stupidity. Fools leading Fools astray, the blind leading the blind.

It is, what it is! Believe it or Not!!!

Chapter Three

From Chaos to Entropy

Swings the Balance of Reality

Understanding the concept of random order is to understand the brilliance of higher cause and effect. The sequence of the I Chin, Astrology, or Numerology are all based on theoretical probability of sequential order and reoccurrence of greatest probability.

NO Magic Just Math.

What will be is always predetermined in the Matrix and only extraordinary effort beyond the course of normality can reprogram the sequence. Once an order of reprogramming the sequence has been established, a new sequence of possibility will be opened to the gamer creating an improved alternate reality than the one previously experienced.

At this point there is either contentment, satisfaction, or boredom left over from the thrill of the game that got you the success that you are now experiencing.

The only pure motivation for success is a quest for greater understanding and a need to be part of the solution and an element in the advancement of our race onward until the achievement of pure unconditional Love is achieved. Everything else is only selfishness.

What one sees as an explosion emanating outward from cosmic center in his place and time in the sequence, I see a an exploded view of Divine perfection racing inward towards unification and wholeness of the One and all. Absolute Entropy

Chapter Four

Meanwhile back at the Ranch

Well regardless of what I know or who I represent in the metaphysical reality, in the three dimensional Holographic physical Earth based reality I was still a 47 year old white guitar player from Texas with Bi polar Disorder and the stage was set for me to start programming the gaming reality myself instead of reacting to random game sequences created by the laws of attraction.

I had knowingly and willingly dropped off of the grid in two parallel dimensions. In the physical reality I had formed an unincorporated nonprofit association that represented the actions and effects of the Cooperate legal entity known as **NATHON Q, DEES** thereby relieving myself of any personal responsibility for the actions of said cooperate entity, in addition; I had been written off by both the Government and the VA as a mentally ill nutcase to be annihilated once Marshall law took effect.

I was left alone as just another bi polar nutcase to be exterminated by the system once the **NATO New World Order** started implementing its population reduction plan.

On the Metaphysical plane I had denounced all religious affiliations and removed myself completely from the false religious Matrix of possibility thereby rendering its cause and effect ineffective. By not acknowledging the existence of a spirit world I destroyed any and all powers and control that it had over me. The greatest way to empower your enemy is to enter into a struggle with them and by simply reasoning away their existence by virtue of a higher understanding; you remove any and all possibility of interferences with said created reality.

So I'm off of both grids and I am free to do my research and work towards fulfilling my destiny with minimum interference from both real and imagined enemies.

Hiding in the Open publicizing, and documenting publically my every move and discrediting any possibility of me being anything other than a Stoned Bi Polar Guitar player from Texas. I said that I was one and created the reality that they perceived me to be.

I delivered myself once again.

Chapter Five

Expanding my Roots

In Costa Rica

I was still living in a small beach town Named "Jaco" on the Central Pacific coastline of Costa Rica. I had become pretty well established in Jaco after having lived there and ran my surfers Hostel for many years. I still lived on the property for free but as the terms of my staying there I could not utilize the facilities for commercial purposes. In a way I feel like that my land lord Floyd was protecting me from myself and allowing me the time that I needed to grow without creating some sort of business. The property was worth about 2.5 million dollars on the current real estate market and Floyd Woods wanted the commercial buildings closed and locked up until he had a cash buyer but I somehow felt all along that I would end up owning the property myself.

The property was only 50 meters from the beach in downtown Jaco and fronted on two main streets. Calle Central and Calle Cocal. It was the home the original "Nathon's Hostel" Building which was vacant but still completely the way that it was the day that my Father Byron closed the doors after losing his eyesight. Next was Floyd's house. Then a very large Restaurant building sitting there vacant with all the equipment in it ready to roll plus a giant built in BBQ Pit and an open fenced in field next door to the OZ Hotel that could easily house a bike rally or concert venue. Behind Floyd's house was my house facing the next street with a back door that accessed the area behind the business where I built my meditation pyramid.

Well having so much potential for possibility and success right there in my own living room and understanding that I couldn't use it was driving me stir crazy to say the least but it is always a lesson in patients and understanding that there is a higher calling and a greater plan for those that have vision.

I built up a PA system and started doing shows and promoting my books and CD's, I bought my neighbors 1970 VW minibus and started restoring it so that I could do road shows. I had everything ready to start a new direction and I got a stop in my spirit and I just sat. In the following week I saw an ad on Face book for a big Esoteric festival near my town called

"Envision" well on my budget there was no way that I could afford the four hundred dollar event ticket. Because of my many skills I was offered a position as volunteer staff as a Bilingual greeter at the front gate of the festival so for four days I met everyone that came in or out and did a tremendous amount of networking. Apparently I made a way bigger splash then I could have ever expected. Ascended teachers, Gurus, Jedi and the like started falling out of trees and after nearly ten years of solitude in Costa Rica I was instantly surrounded by a large permiculture community of esoteric adepts and enlightened souls.

I had a family of friends and people like me once again. Thank You Envision!

Chapter Six

The Envision Festival

Costa Rica

After securing a post at the festival front gate I started to build up anticipation for a paradigm shift or another ascension upgrade at the event so my expectations were high on that point but also on another. You see traditionally being a Jedi much less and Grey Jedi neo Hippy types freak out on me because they don't understand the source of my power or what I represent. I'm sure it's because a big biker guy scared them or something but in Austin my friends and I could walk through the drum circle at Barton Springs to see our friend Richard Garcia and those neo hippy kids would spread like Moses parting the Red sea.

"Nathon Your Crown Chakra Aura is Red and it's filling the whole room" Summer Walters

"Really, I was just thinking about how calm and relaxed that I am, You should see what happens when I turn that shit up sister!" me.

Any way the point is this. I was prepared to be very low key and try not to freak out all the Hippy kids while trapped with them all alone in the jungle and I was sensitive to people's gentleness when I am generally not.

But there were no issues at all. Not being in American society and having the Festival in such a remote location it only attracted people with open enough minds to see past the social barriers and programming that cause such divisions and all of a sudden I was just another free soul experiencing life in unity with others one with nature and free from the oppression of the misguided and misdirected.

Wow what a relief!

I managed to gravitate towards a couple of Jedi my age sitting in the darkness alone by a fire. It was as if no one even knew we were there. With a Word, a sign and I Token I had identified two Masonic brothers and I gave them both a meteorite and a copy of the Book of Nathon and we discussed our current mission at this festival as Observers of Consciousness like spiritual Rangers there to keep the peace on a higher plane and observe and report to source consciousness through our eyes and ears telepathically.

I awoke the first morning and reported for duty bright eyed and bushy tailed at Six AM to the surprise of the volunteer coordinator an hour before my shift so I would be prepared.

Everything at the festival was all built from native Bamboo and the crew that built everything, did a fantastic job. The stage and Lighting was very nice and very creative and the Esprit de Corps and unity of those involved in their projects was a beautiful thing and somewhat restored my hope in the youth of our future being able to return to and embrace the basics of living as a person.

I thought "Wow with an Army of neo hippy kids like this I could "Take over the World!".

There was music and dancing and aerial artist, Body painting and clay body masked nudist, Artist painting portraits live, public speakers and teachers, and venders of hand crafts and organic products. I have been a festival go'er for many years but what was different here was the unified spirit of the people and the lack of egoic representation of class, culture, race, sex, age, nothing. This represented a

World that I wanted to live in, This represented a World that I was willing and capable of creating for myself and others here in Costa Rica, now I just needed to make the right connection and all the doors would be opened for me. I had a new direction.

Chapter Seven

A meeting of New Old Friends

Out of the thousands of people at the Envision Festival it was like I was just floating through and appearing from here and there now and then, time to time. I had lots of close personal friends there from Jaco and I never seen even one of them the whole time and I only made personal one on one contact with about five men all my age and all Jedi. When I met Rhino and he said that it was odd not being involved with the festival or performing or speaking or something, I explained that we were there only to observe and experience.

We had finally earned enough gaming credits to sit back and watch others for once and it was a wonderful thing. He and our traveling companions Thomas, Andrew, Max and Cosmo strolled from camp to camp with me at random telling stories and playing guitar, sharing wisdom and communion of the herb.

Every Camp another story, every meeting a tale of another adventure. Time traveling story tellers awakened and drawn together again to a quickening to bring about transformation.

I had come with no thing and I left with no thing and all was provided by the cosmos. Every time that I was met with a legitimate need there was an immediate provision and I was reciprocating the same. I gave away hundreds of dollars worth of books and CD's as well as a pocket full of meteorites for star children and Jedi.

Everyone giving freely of themselves, Even up to the sound engineer and Chris one of the Host of the Jungle Jam festival in Jaco offering me a ride home.

After I returned to Jaco I immediately was taken out by my increasing Kundalini syndrome and spent the next five days lying on the floor wrenching my neck and spine like a serpent shedding its skin or an insect escaping from its chrysalis. My pineal gland was expanding and my brain cavity was growing and it felt like my head was literally going to explode. I understood that there where energy constrictions in my nervous system but I felt that it was due suffering and only a growing pain in my personal evolution.

Being empathic I had taken my grounding staff with me to the festival and walked bare footed when possible. I would stop at random in certain areas and literally start channeling energy back into the Earth like a cosmic conduit. I did all of this second nature like I had done it many times before but I hadn't. I just knew what to do. A lady even stopped me and told me that she was having problems dealing with all of the energy that was there and I showed her my shamans staff and explained to her how I was channeling the energy through me instead of absorbing it and then I showed her my Metal Ti Chi method of violently forcing out negative energy with one move as opposed to a bunch of stupid ritual. I saw her again later and she was ecstatically thankful and healed.

Anyway, after I recovered I ran some book adds and posted a free copy of some of my work on the Envision site making it known that I was here and that I was interested in teaching young people practical skills and bush craft and I wanted to learn to work with bamboo. I was hoping to make contact with some of the cool folks that I had met at Envision and continue the Envisionment , that's when I had the pleasure of meeting Ms Elena Ross and Finca Amanacer. I had found my small jungle bamboo playground and a 17 year old Hippy girl from the 60's that owned her own little piece of heaven and needed a space cowboy to run her cosmic ranch. I was one of five players that she needed to fulfill her vision or change direction because she was tired and had done all that she could do with the limited skill sets of youth volunteers.

Chapter Eight
Going Home to a
Place I've never been before
Finca Amanacer Londres, Costa Rica

Elena had posted on the Envision site soliciting specific individuals interested in co creating a small self sustained permiculture community and mentioning her Hostel and events that the finca sponsored in the past such as the Burning Spirit Festival so I responded.

In a bizarre twist of singularity when I posted my book on the Envision site that she had read, it had somehow posted it backwards as if that is even possible, so this first thing that she read was the last page in the book "Things my Daddy Told Me" and she wanted to meet the man that wrote that and see if he was real or not.

Ms Elena was a tall slender lady in her sixties and quite an anomaly herself.

I could tell that she was well versed and educated and had been somewhat of a socialite, sailing the oceans in yachts and mingling with the rich and famous but yet she had left all that behind years ago for the dream of her own hippy commune where she could enjoy nature and share peace and love with others.

She was a visionary and with no husband, boyfriend or tagalongs to help her she had single handedly pursued this specific finca for years and bought it, paid for it, and turned it into a working flow through campgrounds and hostel using labor from volunteer traveler programs and hiring local laborers for cash. Everything else was on bartering for room and meals to enjoy the facilities that she had provided. So for nearly a decade she was running a seven acre perpetual summer camp for kids that would rather goof off for four hours volunteering than pay for a room and meal so that they could buy weed and beer and doing it all by herself minus the aid of a weekly housekeeper.

I could see where that I was greatly needed there and that I could help her shift into the next level of being a learning and performance center teaching people how to create sustainability and live in small communal farms working together with each other and the environment. I could build a few Earth ships from bamboo and show others how. I could build irrigation systems with perpetual hydraulic ram pumps creating electricity with Pelton wheel generators moved by the irrigation flow. Aquaponic tanks raising fish to eat and creating biospheres for aerobic waste water treatment system and plant nutrients. I could center the homes around one central utility building that provided steam, hot showers, a communal kitchen, waste water and electricity as well as laundry facilities. Elena had personally planted enough bamboo to continually harvest it and have an unlimited supply of construction material on the farm.

It looked as if all I needed to do was just DoIt! Everything was set in place.
All of the characters were manifesting themselves one by one and Elena's all star Jedi team was slowly coming together. We were all being led to teach the chosen how to sustain themselves in a post New World Order Earth and usher in the dawning of a New Age.

Chapter Nine
Strange things are amiss
At the Circle K Dude

So I keep a strict diet of no spiritualism as to say to prevent from being blinded by the false reality of the war in heaven in the matrix of religious reality, so I thought that I was more or less safe around the New Age community, esoteric, and pagans but I was quick to learn that this world was another cookie cutter archetype of the same Christian world of delusional thinking and dogma that I had already delivered myself from.

There were wealthy clueless tree huggers from San Francisco yacht clubs forming commercial esoteric communities for money, and spreading bad information and playing with spiritual forces that they know absolutely nothing about.

There were mentally ill people that ran to an environment where their skewed perceptions of reality and schizophrenia were accepted as higher spiritual understanding and gifts.

There were burned out Terrance McKenna Hippies that had dropped one too many hits of acid or did that hundredth mushroom trip on an Ayahuaska journey and lost touch with a practical and functional reality.

And there were young, lost victims of social programming with ADD and Bi Polar disorder with no direction and no one to lead them to the light of true understanding.

A virtual island of misfit toys that I had to dodge, and work around in order to help the chosen few that had a clue.

There is just no nice way to put this. Some people are just too fucking stupid to help and you waist valuable time that could have been used helping someone with real potential for change.

But more amazingly I kept running into Jedi and Gaming characters that I knew from past realities and meeting a lot of people that really did know what's going on and were up to speed camouflaged amongst the flakes, fruits and nuts.
Former military people, marshal artist, Yoga instructors, indigenous shamans, teachers, free masons, and initiates in the mystery schools. I had found people that I could relate to and respect. Finally people

that I could learn from share with and grow as an individual.

We were separating ourselves from the Government infiltrated mind control camps and were forming an Occult underground of knowledge and a mystery school right under their noses and providing an alternate path to those that were drawn in that direction in the never ending quest for higher light and understanding.
It was the birth of a new Jedi order in the ubiquitous plight against the Archonic forces of darkness that were set in motion for the eradication of human life on Earth and the prevention of the evolution of humankind.

Chapter Ten
Walk-ins/Check-outs
And the Return to Witch Mountain

So I'm told that there is a really neat kid that I ought to meet that has been at the finca but had left for a few days to attend and esoteric séance at a nearby New age Cult community Called Bear Mountain Ranch.
Well I didn't go to the event because I really do try and avoid any and all forms of said organizational religious practice and spiritual gatherings just because of the extreme amount of ignorance that is so prominent among New Agers.

As always this was a wise decision.

When I met this kid for the first time he addressed himself as Day....Vid (in a Robot

Voice) and he said that my presence had lifted him from his great darkness. I looked him strait in his Dark overshadowed eyes and I said "I can see that, you look like you are Demon possessed Dude, I've seen it before. In response to this remark he dropped down prone in front of me and started calling me master and I looked at my friend and said "What in the Fuck is Wrong with this kid and how long has he been this way?"

Come to find out that days earlier when he had first arrived before leaving for Bear Mountain Ranch he was a perfectly normal 26 year old Cocky kid from Alabama and was bright, happy and perfectly normal and now I had a completely manic schizophrenic experiencing absolutely delusional multiple personality disorder Or I had a Walk-in.

Well being the non spiritual guy that I am I asked one of the ladies that was traveling with him if they were doing stupid ass rituals and séances at Bear Mountain with Dave. "They did a spirit Cleansing"
Well then you better take this kid back there and find out who is responsible for this mess because as far as I'm concerned this walk in is an alien hostile and this Kid Dave's soul is being held captive in another dimension and someone has some explaining to do. Within Minutes she was on the phone with the other ladies that were there and they had pinpointed the exact ritual and moment that the kid had checked out.
By the next day a Bear Mountain Occultist had arrived to pick up the kid and shelter him somewhere until they could figure out what to do with him.
She had the same overshadowed dark eyes and when she came to get him she looked

me strait in the face and said to Elena "This is all Nathon's fault! You have changed Elena, everything has changed since he arrived, this is all his fault".

Well I laughed my ass off at that statement realizing that the only thing that I had done wrong was directly address a very serious issue concerning a young man's mental and spiritual health when every other Guru and enlightened person there was acting like it was an elephant room and I wasn't supposed to point out that this kid was following me around worshiping me and calling me Lucifer, His mage, His muse, His master. Hell I not only pointed it out I directly addressed the issue publicly in front of the whole hostel when I turned tu him and said "Archon, where is David and what have you done with him?" to which he responded "David is Dead and he is not coming back".

Well there you go you dumb ass spiritualist with your stupid Angel cards and séances. You need to call this guys fiancé and his parents and explain to them that David is never coming home because you wanted to have a cleansing.

The dangers of playing with things that you truly don't understand.

"Ok my Esoteric Hippy Wannabe Padawons. When you leave your house you lock and secure it. When you leave your Car you lock, Secure and set an Alarm! So then Why in the Fuck would you get with a bunch of untrained unprofessional New Age Idiots practicing things that they don't understand in such blissful ignorance and be cohersed into having an out of body experience??? Almost All of the mentally ill / Demon Possessed / Walk in Victims that I am forced to deal with have one thing in common. They usually invited the

damn thing in on their own and therefore I
have very little compassion for them at all and
even less authority to deal with said issue
because the victim knowingly and willingly left
his or her body unattended while they went on
a cosmic sightseeing tour. This is really about
the stupidest thing that any human could ever
do on their own. You will have plenty of out of
body time when your Earth Suit is Dead so I
highly recommend that you stay in the
muthafucker until it stops working.
It is as Stupid as leaving your car parked
downtown with the keys in it and the engine
running with your wallet, ID and a full tank of
fuel. When you consider the risk involved in
such unnecessary spiritual practice as
opposed to any benefits if there are any you
will realize that you are being DUPED and SET
UP for FAILURE by Malevolent Cocksuckers
that do not care about your spiritual identity or
personal well being. Invasion of the Body
Snatchers all over again!
In Closing You create this reality through your
own beliefs and then Butt Fuck Yourselves by

creating the very reality that enslaves you to
Darkness."

Chapter Eleven
The Harsh Reality at Hand

Every since I wrote my first book "Satan
God or Schizzo" I had avoided the war of
the Spirits and just focused on my own well
being and mental health. Now does that
mean that I am ignorant of the devices of
that gaming matrix? God forbid.

Now since I was following it as an outside
observer viewing it from the prospective of
a allegorical story instead of an actual
belief system, teaching me the balances of
Light and darkness, Good and evil, or any
other polar opposites that demonstrate to
us the need for balance unity and harmony

in our virtual existence, it had no effect on me and I never entered into that matrix of reality.

Now I was dealing with damaged psyches again that were operating under these constraints making me subject to these delusive perspectives of reality.

Every time that I met a seeker operating under this flawed theology I was harrowed as being a being of divine light or in fact Lucifer himself. Well all ego aside, I'm the one that gets a crazy check and you have a bachelors degree in theology, but yet I proclaim to know nothing and just be a guy with Bi Polar Disorder but you claim that I am a supernatural demigod? Now who is the crazy one? Hell even if I was Lucifer "which is in fact the single most ludicrous thing that I have ever heard"

I'm still trapped in the same damn gaming matrix as you and I obviously do not have any spiritual super powers or I would be a World Famous super millionaire Rock Star and your old lady would be blowing me.

I refused to enter into this world of imagination for my own amusement but yet I was forced to for the benefit of those held captive by the lies of religious confusion and dogma created realities of fear and ignorance.

The only way to remove this bad programming is with the same program that got it there in the first place.
At which point it is just simply more efficient to Call upon this imaginary authority to take control over the imaginary spirits that are causing the imaginary struggle that you have chose to participate in out of your own ignorance usually.
Screw That!!! This is what I'm going to do.

I will write an instructional manual explaining in great detail how I overcame this delusional reality and delivered myself from the manipulative mind control of the Archons and if you need spiritual counseling you can buy my book and read it.

Otherwise I have realized that only those that seek find, and the door is only opened to those that knock, and the mysteries of the universe are only a mystery to those that look outside of themselves for the answers.

The End

Thank You
Nathon Dees

Thank You and Pura Vida, N8

Please check out my other Books and Music

@ REVNATHONDEES.COM